PACEWALKING

PACEWALKING

The Balanced Way to Aerobic Health

Steven Jonas, M.D.,
and
Peter Radetsky
Illustrated by Valerie A. Kells

Crown Publishers, Inc.
New York

For Irvin "Kim" Korr, Ph.D., Charles Ogilvie, D.O.,
Ralph Willard, D.O.,
and the
Texas College of Osteopathic Medicine

Publisher's Note: This book contains exercise and diet instructions to be followed within the context of an overall health program. However, not all exercises and dietary recommendations are designed for every individual. Before starting this or any other exercise and/or diet program a physician should be consulted. The instructions in this book are not intended as a substitute for professional medical advice.

Library of Congress Cataloging-in-Publication Data
Jonas, Steven.
    PaceWalking: the balanced way to aerobic health/Steven Jonas and Peter Radetsky.
    p.   cm.
    Includes index.
    1. Walking—Health aspects.   2. Physical fitness.   I. Radetsky,
Peter.   II. Title.   III. Title: Pace walking.
RA781.65.J66   1988   87-31857
613.7'1—dc 19   CIP

ISBN 0-517-56809-8
10 9 8 7 6 5 4 3 2 1
First Edition

Contents

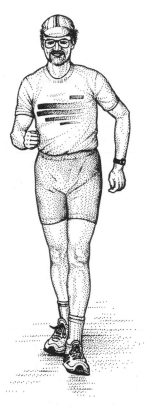

Preface

*T*his book is about a sport that I call PaceWalking. PaceWalking is aerobic walking for exercise and health. Every able-bodied person walks; it is as basic as eating, sleeping, and breathing. But PaceWalking is a purposeful, planned athletic activity that you do because you *choose* to do it.

PaceWalking is one of the Big Five of the aerobic sports. The others are running, cycling, swimming, and aerobic dancing. PaceWalking gives you the same benefits of health and fitness as the other aerobic sports, when done at the same level of intensity for the same period of time.

The philosophy of PaceWalking has several general principles, which I come back to from time to time throughout the book. If you are like me, you probably won't read a book like this one from cover to cover. You will pick out those sections that are of particular interest and use to you. I repeat my major points from time to time because I want to make sure that all readers see them at least once, even if they read only parts of the book.

Balance is one of those themes. So is *goal-setting*. I feel strongly that whatever you do in exercise, you must do it because, deep down inside, you want to do it for yourself.

A principle basic to any PaceWalking program is consistency and regularity. *Consistency* means that the amount of time you spend in each training session should not vary too much from week to week. *Regularity* means that you spread your training sessions out evenly; you don't cram all your exercise into the weekend and do nothing on the weekdays, for instance. The body doesn't take too kindly to inconsistency or irregularity.

I talk about PaceWalking as being good for the heart, uplifting to the spirit, and easy on the body. PaceWalking has all the advantages for health and feeling good that other aerobic sports have, but it has virtually none of their disadvantages. Indeed, I call PaceWalking the Foundation Aerobic SporT: F.A.S.T. Once you become a PaceWalker, you have established an aerobic base from which you can do any of the other aerobic sports that suits you. In chapter 8 I describe an aerobic exercise schedule called PaceTraining, in which a program in two or more sports is built upon the F.A.S.T.

This book explains in detail what PaceWalking is. It provides day-by-day and week-by-week training programs. It shows you the PaceWalking technique and gives you advice on equipment. It has information about PaceWalking and the older person and PaceWalking for the pregnant woman. It tells you how, if you want to, you can get into racing as a PaceWalker. It presents the scientific evidence that clearly demonstrates the link between regular leisure-time exercise and good health, and it discusses some important information about nutrition. It will help you—if you want to— to become a PaceWalker.

CHAPTER 1

An Introduction

Walking. It's the simplest activity in the world—you just put one foot in front of the other, and you're off. No difficult techniques to learn, no expensive equipment to buy. But although walking is our basic means of moving about, until recently people haven't walked for exercise—aerobic exercise, that is. Go out and stretch the legs, walk off dinner, take a stroll with friends, yes. But walk to get in shape? To firm up and maybe lose a few pounds? To get the heart beating and tone the body? No, these were tasks best left to other activities: running, swimming, bicycling, aerobic dancing. And if walking were involved at all, it was something you did afterwards, to cool down or mellow out.

Yes, it's true that there were—and still are—people who took walking seriously, who even competed as intensely as any runner ever has. Race walkers, they're called. But for most people, the thought of race walking conjures up little more than a complicated series of movements—a tricky, hip-swinging gait accompanied by pronounced arm movements. The activity was fulfilling for some, but it remained on the fringes of the sporting world. The gait was technically difficult; to learn it demanded real effort and commitment. It was something that a few people did, and most of us know of it primarily through brief glimpses on television around Olympics time. Race walking never percolated down into the burgeoning fitness movement, as competitive running has. The fitness boom boomed right past walking. This most basic of activities was odd man out.

All that has changed. Now walking—not race walking, but just plain old walking—has taken its rightful place among aerobic activities. Walking gear has become a big business. Walking magazines are showing up on the newsstands. And well-known advocates of other aerobic exercises are giving walking their wholehearted endorsements. Says running enthusiast George Sheehan,

> Walking is the best exercise of all. It requires little or no instruction. . . . Walking is also virtually free of injury. . . . Walking is a gentle, effective way to become fit.

But what has caused walking finally to become recognized as a good—maybe even the best—aerobic exercise?

One answer may be that other popular activities have for one reason or another begun to disenchant people a bit. For example, to swim you need a pool—or an ocean or lake, which are even less accessible for most of us. To bicycle you need a bike and a safe, convenient place to ride it (unless you use a stationary bike—that's another story). And unless you're uncommonly independent, to do aerobic dance you must join a class; if nothing else, that means money and going back and forth to a club. In other words, because of necessary equipment or location or cost, each of these activities is in its own way inconvenient. To run, of course, you need nothing but a good pair of shoes—and not even that if you run on the beach. But many people are finding that although running is convenient and demands very little in terms of equipment, it's just plain tough—certainly not for everyone. And more than that, running can be hard on the runner who overdoes it. More injuries result from running than any other sport. The growing field of sports medicine in large part owes its health to unhealthy runners.

So, what's a body to do? You want to exercise, want to get in shape, want to improve the quality of your life. For many, the answer is Walk. It's as convenient as running—even more so, since you can walk just about anywhere—and it's accessible and inexpensive. Walking is an activity that virtually anyone—*anyone*—can do, and at any age. It demands little in the way of physical conditioning to start with, and it promotes less wear and tear and has less potential for injury than any other aerobic sport. It demands relatively little in the way of skill and attention to technique. And—here's the best part—when done correctly and at a proper level of intensity, walking can be as effective as any other exercise in promoting aerobic health. Neither running, nor swimming, nor bicycling, nor aerobic dancing, nor any other activity will put you in better aerobic condition than PaceWalking, when all are done at the same intensity. Your heart can't distinguish among various aerobic sports. It doesn't care what you do as long as you keep it beating. And when you move large muscles in a regular rhythmic fashion, your heart must beat faster and pump more blood with each beat. Raised to a certain minimum level, that heart rate becomes aerobic.

But you can't just go out for a Sunday stroll and expect to realize aerobic benefits. Nothing comes that easily. You have to work at it a little, be concerned with pace and duration. You have to get your heart beating to the point where it'll do you some good. What follows is a suggestion on just how to do that, with a minimum of fuss and a maximum of fun. I call it PaceWalking.

PaceWalking—Who Is It For?

It's easy enough to say that PaceWalking is for everyone. I believe that to be true. But it might be a good idea to pinpoint potential PaceWalkers. If you find yourself in one of these categories, take heed; PaceWalking just might be the sport for you.

New Exercisers

Let's say you've never exercised regularly before, and you've decided the time has come. All well and good. Now what do you do? Here's this bewildering array of choices. The local health club has been sending you advertisements in the mail, you see pods of cyclists along the side of the road every weekend, runners pound the pavement outside the office during lunch breaks, the sporting goods stores are jammed with swim suits, tennis outfits, aerobic clothes. Where should you start?

If you're like most people, you decide to give running a try. It's cheap, accessible, and requires little in the way of technique or training. But you soon find that running is demanding. It's tough. And it hurts. For most new runners, the sport doesn't become fun until at least a month has gone by. "Who needs it?" you decide. There are other ways to torture yourself.

So you try alternatives. Aerobic dance sounds great, but the class is so crowded. And besides, you don't like the way you look in tights and don't like having to be at the club at 8:00 in the morning to take the class. Swimming? Out of the question. Water in your eyes and nose and ears is not your idea of fun, and battling the splashing hordes for lane space is even less appealing. Cycling? That means getting a bike, and that means money.

Well, here's a modest proposal: Try PaceWalking. It's cheap. The only mandatory purchase is a good pair of shoes. You can wear whatever you want—most likely you already have a suitable outfit hanging in the closet. It can be done anywhere, and at any time. You don't have to wait in any lines or fight crowds to PaceWalk. And it doesn't hurt, at least not like running hurts. It feels natural, comfortable. Why didn't you think of it before?

As you'll see in chapter 4, the PaceWalking Program (PWP) proceeds at a very easy pace. In fact, you're in complete control of the pace of your training. For the beginner, the only commitment that PaceWalking requires is that of a very modest amount of time.

And you can PaceWalk indefinitely—you'll need no other aerobic exercise—or you can use it as a foundation to move into other exercise activities. I call it the Foundation Aerobic SporT—F.A.S.T., for short. For example, if you still want to eventually be a runner, PaceWalking provides a perfect beginning. It gets you used to exercising regularly, and it builds up your aerobic capabilities and your muscle strength. If you start from no athletic background at all, your chances of becoming a runner—or a cyclist or, certainly, a triathlete—are especially good if you work into it through PaceWalking. For the nonexerciser, PaceWalking is a terrific way to start.

The Current Walker

Many people walk, but relatively few realize aerobic benefits from walking. That is, although walking may be a pleasure, it may not be doing much for your health or level of fitness.

That's where PaceWalking comes in. It's different from strolling or hiking or marathon walking. It's different from merely picking up your pace while walking to work. PaceWalking turns this most natural of activities—walking—into an aerobically beneficial exercise.

If you already walk and are interested in getting the most out of what may be an occasional activity by formalizing it and making it something you do on a regular basis and for a particular purpose—that means PaceWalking. If you walk but aren't sure that what you're doing is aerobic, or if you wish you "belonged" to a certain sport, PaceWalking may be for you. It's a way of doing what comes naturally and benefiting from it at the same time.

The Aspiring and Irregular Aerobic Athlete

Some people try a variety of aerobic activities but never stick with any one. Their exercise experience is a history of starts and stops—the former full of enthusiasm and high expectations, the latter laced with disillusionment and dashed hopes. It's a pattern that can become tiresome, until finally it's not worth trying at all.

The reasons for this lack of aerobic success are many: the cost of exercising, the inconvenience, the difficulty, the pain, the injury, and the plain lack of enjoyment in the doing. And the same reasons may turn a regular aerobic exerciser into an irregular one. It just isn't worth the trouble.

If any of these descriptions fit, PaceWalking may be for you. And besides its own intrinsic value, PaceWalking is an ideal lead-in for any number of aerobic activities. It can serve as the foundation for a more varied exercise program, perhaps involving those very sports you tried, and quit, before. You may be able to utilize that closetful of little-used equipment and clothing after all.

The Injured Aerobic Athlete

There are two categories of injuries in aerobic sports. I call one *intrinsic*, the other *extrinsic*.

Intrinsic injuries are those that arise from *within* the body and are usually caused by overuse. The body can only take so much pounding, twisting, swiveling, contracting, and expanding. After a while something has to give. We experience that breakdown as pain, swelling, and loss of strength and range of motion.

These are injuries most associated with running (there are more injuries from running than from any other aerobic activity—which is understandable since there are more runners than other kinds of aerobic exercisers), and they go by names like tendinitis, shin splints, muscle strains and tears, and stress fractures.

Extrinsic injuries come from the *outside* and are most common in cycling. A flat tire, a broken spoke, hitting a pothole in the road, running into an immovable object, being thrown off the bike by an irresistible force—all of these can, and often do, cause injuries. And the other aerobic sports have their own variety of extrinsic injuries.

So there's a small army of wounded aerobic exercisers limping around out there, chomping at the bit to *do* something, but unable to get back to the activity that wounded them in the first place. If you're one of these unfortunate people, PaceWalking might well be the ideal exercise for you—as an interim method of staying in shape while you're waiting to go back to your original activity, or as a complementary or replacement exercise in itself. For the injury risk in PaceWalking, intrinsic or extrinsic, is very low. If your particular injury isn't aggravated by the motion of PaceWalking, you can pretty well walk assured that you'll not hurt yourself further.

And, remember, you'll realize similar health and fitness benefits from PaceWalking as you would from any other aerobic activity done at the same intensity level for the same period of time. As for your cardiovascular system, you'll lose nothing.

The Burned-Out Case

Finally, if you're burned-out from your usual aerobic sport—can't stand the thought of lacing on the running shoes, or climbing onto the bike, or diving into the pool even one more time—PaceWalking may be for you. Too much time spent training, too much intensity, perhaps even too much competition—any of these can cause burn-out.

The result is that you're bored, even depressed. You can't stand to keep going as you have, but you can't stop either. Anyone who has been hooked—and burned-out—on aerobic exercise knows that, as depressing as it may be to continue, it's even more depressing to stop. It's like an addiction; your body can't do without it.

PaceWalking may be the treatment. It's aerobic but not too intense. It's relatively pain free. It can involve competing but with no chance of winning. You can't go as fast as the runners. You can't go as fast as the race walkers. So the monkey of having to perform at a certain level is off your back. You can realize aerobic benefits with no pressure and perhaps gradually recover from your burn-out. And, if nothing else, you'll have the great pleasure of actually *enjoying* exercise once again.

PaceWalking as Aerobic Exercise—
Why Do It at All?

The idea of aerobic exercise is at the heart of the entire fitness movement. It's what took the possibility of life-enhancing exercise out of the realm of the exceptionally dedicated and plunked it right into the laps of all the rest of us. No longer is it necessay to knock yourself out at some daunting exercise regime to improve the quality of your life. The appeal of aerobic exercise is that, if you can improve your heart's ability to pump blood, and therefore your body's ability to utilize what the blood provides—life-giving oxygen—you'll be healthier as a result. And to be healthy means to function as well as you possibly can, to stay well, and to keep the risk of illness as low as possible.

The key is just what the word *aerobic*—from the Greek for "air" and "life"—suggests: In aerobics you want to exercise your heart and you want to breathe. But that doesn't mean any of this panting, gasping, out-of-breath business. None of that working out until you drop. In aerobic exercise, you don't go for the burn, you go for the heartbeats. Aerobic exercise involves doing any rhythmic, repetitive activity that involves one or more major muscle group at a pace that forces your heart rate into the "aerobic range"—more on that in a minute. In aerobic exercise, the energy that your muscles use is supplied by burning the oxygen in air breathed in, rather than using your body's own limited supply of stored energy.

The results are well worth it. Aerobic exercise helps lower your blood pressure and cholesterol levels. It strengthens your cardiovascular system, thereby decreasing your risk of heart attack. (In 1987, the U.S. Public Health Service concluded that *lack* of exercise actually *increases* the risk of heart attack.) In time it even changes your metabolism so you can burn accumulated fat for energy. That means that the calories you use in exercise come more readily from your spare tire than your lunch. Aerobic exercise will help you do other active things more effectively, even if those things consist of nothing more than climbing the stairs to the office or the second story of your home. There's evidence that it raises your overall life expectancy. And, what's most important to many people, aerobic exercise just plain makes you feel better.

All this from exercising your heart and breathing. Pretty slick. And the thing is, *anything* that exercises your heart will do the deed. When many people think of aerobic exercise the activities that come to mind are four of the Big Five: running, cycling, swimming, and aerobic dancing. These are demanding, vigorous, high-energy activities that make you work. Well, they can be good aerobic conditioners, it's true. But your heart doesn't know if you're running or dancing or cycling or swimming. All it knows is that it's being forced to beat quickly enough to circulate enough blood to supply the oxygen your hard-working body needs. And if another activity forces it to beat as quickly and for as long a stretch, that activity is every bit as effective an aerobic conditioner. Aerobic conditioning does *not* have to be violent or demanding or wearing. All it has to do is force your heart to beat at a certain rate for a certain time.

What is an aerobic heart rate? It's easy: 70 to 85 percent of your maximum heart rate, for at least twenty minutes, three times a week. In other words, all you need to do to achieve the benefits of aerobic exercise is to walk at least three times a week, for at least twenty minutes each time, keeping your heart rate at 70 to 85 percent of its maximum.

Of course anything less than that won't hurt. There's nothing magic about twenty minutes three times a week, it's just a guide. Fifteen minutes will help. Ten minutes is better than nothing. But the American College of Sports Medicine has determined that at least twenty minutes three times a week will give consistent health benefits from exercise.

Now you're ready to start. The next step is to figure out what heart rate to sustain, and then how best to get your heart beating that fast in the first place. The first part can be satisfied with a simple formula—I'll talk about it in detail in chapter 3 (see page 26). The second is what this book is all about.

CHAPTER 2

PaceWalking—
The Roots of Success

To become a successful PaceWalker, first you must know *why.* *Why* do you want to exercise? Your reasons for exercising help determine your goals—*what* you want to get out of it—which in turn lead to your methods—*how* you go about it. Why, then what and how.

Knowing Why

In my own case, my interest in exercise grew out of how I wanted people to see me. I was concerned about my image.

It was the spring of 1980. Here I was, forty-three years old, a professor of preventive medicine, and I didn't exercise. So what? I wasn't unhappy not exercising. As a doctor, I knew that I wasn't particularly out of shape or unhealthy. I had never smoked, and I rarely drank. My blood pressure was actually on the low side. I wasn't *too* overweight—in fact, I had just lost ten pounds. My diet was fairly high in fat and cholesterol, but I didn't feel myself to be at an especially high risk for cardiovascular disease, cancer, or any of the other major killers. And I was a good fellow. I helped old ladies across the street and wore my seat belt.

But I felt that it just didn't look good for someone who espoused preventing medical problems not to practice what he preached. Exercise is simply the most visible health and fitness activity. And besides, I had just begun working as a consultant in preventive medicine and medical education at the Texas College of Osteopathic Medicine in Forth Worth. Many of my colleagues there exercised and were in pretty good shape. I was conspicuous by my absence on the running path or in the gym. So I started thinking about developing an exercise program for myself. I was sure that I would hate it, but it would be good for my image to be able to say that I exercised regularly. And, after all, I had heard that twenty minutes three times a week were the magic numbers; that didn't seem too bad.

So I thought about it. And I thought about it. Through the summer and fall I thought about it. And I did nothing.

Then in October I had my moment of truth. I was in Detroit for a meeting. It took place at Cobo Hall, a large arena whose floors are connected to one another by ramps. During the first morning I walked up a story on one of those ramps, and by the time I got to the top I was out of breath, huffing and puffing. Well, by now the exercise seed had been planted in my mind. Whereas before I might have accepted my lack of wind simply as one of the by-products of middle age, I found that I could no longer tolerate it. "Enough is enough," I said to myself. "When I get home, I'm starting."

For me the decision to start exercising stemmed finally from dissatisfaction with my physical condition. That's the best kind of reason, actually, because it comes from within. There's nobody telling you to get going, nobody putting pressure on from the outside. You simply *want* to exercise because you don't like yourself the way you are. I didn't *like* getting out of breath so easily, and I vowed that it would never happen again. I wanted to become aerobically fit. So I started running.

It took me a couple of weeks before I could even run twenty minutes without stopping, but soon I was doing my twenty minutes, three times a week. And what's more, I found that I *liked* it. I bought my first pair of running shoes, and my workouts started getting longer. In the summer of 1981 I bought a ten-speed bike to add some variety to my training program. On Memorial Day 1982, I entered my first race, a five-mile run. The next year I ran a marathon and, having added swimming to my repertoire, competed in my first two triathlons.

I never finished first or even placed in my age class—I never came close. But I finished, and I loved every minute of it—well, almost every minute. A former nonathlete who didn't have the hand-eye coordination for baseball or basketball or tennis, I had become an athlete in my forties. And an enthusiastic one, at that.

Exercise has changed my self-image as well as the way people see me. I feel good on a day-to-day basis. I feel stimulated and up from the exercise itself. I've explored my limits, and I recognize my limitations. I know I'm not going to go really fast—I just enjoy finishing. And when I beat my own estimated time for a race, I really feel fantastic.

What does all this have to do with PaceWalking? Well, in September of 1985 I was pounding away in the running leg of the Cape Cod Endurance Triathlon. I had already completed the 2.4-mile swim and the 112-mile bike leg. Twenty-six more miles to go. My goal was to finish within the seventeen-hour time limit, but I knew that I just wasn't going to be able to run the whole way. So I decided to run for ten minutes, then walk for ten minutes, run for ten minutes, walk for ten minutes, and so on, conserving my strength until I crossed the finish line.

Finally, I came to the last stretch of the race. It was dark and getting cold, and my legs were killing me. So I just stopped running and walked the rest of the way. And I did it—I finished within the time limit. That's when I started thinking seriously about walking for exercise.

Walking. Less is more. You don't have to beat yourself into the ground to realize aerobic benefits from this particular exercise. I added walking to my training regimen and soon I was walking half marathons and the running legs of triathlons. I gradually learned the technique I describe in chapter 3, coined the term, "PaceWalking," and came up with the idea for this book.

I've learned that PaceWalking does just what any good aerobic exercise does: It promotes health, lifts your mood, and makes you feel better about yourself. It's also fun.

But mine are not the only reasons to start PaceWalking. Some people do it to look better. Some do it to meet people. Some do it because a spouse or friend or boss hounds them until they take the first step. And some do it, as I originally did, for reasons of image; I wanted people to think that I was practicing what I preached.

But in a way there are no wrong reasons to begin. If it's your looks you're concerned with, in time you *will* look better because PaceWalking will help reduce your body fat and build up your muscles. In contrast to fat, muscles can be toned and developed. If it's weight that bothers you, PaceWalking will make losing weight much easier than if you try to do it through diet alone. If you are a smoker or a heavy drinker, PaceWalking can help you deal with those problems by increasing your overall fitness and making you less reliant on smoking and drinking as social functions or stress relievers. PaceWalking can be a particularly good way to help reduce stress.

PaceWalking can indeed help you make new friends. People who do aerobic exercise on a regular basis generally are fit, trim, and attractive. Many people who PaceWalk welcome having partners. And it's especially easy to meet fellow exercisers if you join a walking or running club or do some racing (see chapter 7 for a discussion of the racing PaceWalker). During races, surprisingly enough, the atmosphere is often even more congenial and relaxed than it is out on the PaceWalking path.

The more your reasons come from within, however, rather than from urgings of others, the greater the probability that you will become a regular PaceWalker. For example, if you're exercising in order to please others and you run into problems maintaining your schedule, dealing with bad weather, or handling some minor injury, you may well start blaming those others for the fact that you're stuck with this unpleasant activity. Placing blame can lead to real frustration. Sometimes the easiest way to deal with that frustration is to stop the activity altogether.

If, on the other hand, you're PaceWalking because *you* want to, you'll find it much easier to deal with any problems that may arise. If you're exercising primarily for your own benefit (although others certainly may be pleased with what you're doing), it's easier to stick with it when things get hard. Instead of bailing out, you have a tendency to solve problems.

So try to be sure from the beginning just *why* it is that you're interested in PaceWalking. Again, no reason is the wrong one. You simply want to figure out what yours is.

Setting Realistic Goals

That done, you can move to the next step: setting goals for yourself. But it's important that these goals be realistic ones. You're not going to drop ten pounds overnight. Neither are you going to firm up that sagging belly or those jiggling thighs right away. And a beginning PaceWalker isn't going to step right out and walk a mile in fifteen minutes. Moreover, there's no reason to want to.

Here are a couple of things to remember. First, just as PaceWalking is a relatively gentle and relaxed aerobic activity, the rate at which you realize its benefits is gentle and relaxed as well. You don't want to rush things—moreover, you can't rush them and still expect to get good results from your exercise. You must begin gradually and improve gradually (in chapter 4, the detailed schedules will suggest exactly how). And second, how far and how fast you walk may have *nothing* to do with the quality of your workout. The *pace* of PaceWalking has to do with heart rate. Any pace that moves your heart rate into the aerobic range is the right pace for you. When you first begin, that pace may be little more than a lazy stroll. Or, if you're in pretty good shape to begin with, it may be brisk. The point is that it all depends on you. PaceWalking is an activity that's truly individual.

A reasonable objective for a beginning PaceWalker may be simply to get on a regular schedule of workouts, twenty minutes in length at the minimum. You may not reach the aerobic pace for a few weeks—that's okay. It's developing the habit, and the *feeling*, of working out regularly that's important at first. The rest will come.

Allotting Yourself Enough Time

PaceWalking doesn't take too much time—the average PaceWalker will spend two to three hours per week working out— but even that much time is hard for some people to come by. If you're holding down a full-time job and going to school at night, say, you simply may not have the time to become a PaceWalker, at least not right now.

On the other hand, many people—perhaps even most of us— can make time if they really want to badly enough. It comes down to priorities. It may be that the extra few minutes in bed, or the second cup of coffee, or the drawn-out discussions around the water cooler at work aren't as important as a half hour devoted to your workout. And it may be that the TV soap opera or talk show has to go, so that you can get out and exercise. People who *really* want to, even the busiest people, somehow find time to exercise— expecially since the benefits can be so important.

For example, exercise—not a lot, but a regular program—is so important to me that I work out my weekly, monthly, and even yearly schedules to leave space for exercise. I even record my work-out schedule for each day in my daily calendar: 7:00 to 7:30, PaceWalk. That's A.M., by the way. I'm a morning workout person. I like the feeling of getting ready for the day that a morning workout affords me. And since my calendar also tells me how much time I'll be exercising the next day, I make sure I go to bed early enough to get a good night's sleep and still wake up bright and early for my workout.

There's no consensus on what time of day is best for exercising, though. Dr. Kenneth Cooper, director of the Aerobics Institute in Dallas, and the inventor of the term "aerobics," points out that a workout before the evening meal will actually reduce your appetite. Because exercise increases the amount of sugar in your blood, mimicking the effect of a good meal, it tricks your brain into reading your food level as "full." People exercising to lose weight might find this feature especially attractive.

But if you just can't spare the time, *on a regular basis*, it may not be worth your while even to begin. All that faces you are fits and starts and the frustration of never being able to give it your all. And people who only exercise intermittently, even if that exercise is something as gentle as PaceWalking, run a higher risk of injury than those who work out regularly. If you don't have the time, put this book aside until you do. You'll be a lot happier for it.

The Importance of Consistency and Regularity

Now we're getting down to it. If PaceWalking is going to do you any good at all, you must be consistent and regular in your approach. Let's go into the qualities one at a time.

Consistency refers to the relative lengths of the individual workout sessions. You can't develop aerobic fitness if the length of your workout sessions varies widely. The body just doesn't respond well to such an approach. It likes consistent, predictable workouts—workouts that drive the heart rate into the aerobic range for a long enough time to matter, but not so long as to be detrimental.

For example, if you're following the Introductory PaceWalking Program (see chapter 4) and averaging an hour and a half of exercise a week, it's important that the hour and a half be spaced out over sessions of relatively equal length—that is, no one session more than ten to twenty minutes longer than any other—as the schedule suggests. That way you exercise your heart long enough and often enough so that the effects are lasting. But if you divide that hour and a half into, say, a ten-minute workout one day, a sixty-minute workout next time, and a twenty-minute workout the next, you've done yourself little if any good. The ten-minute session isn't much more than a warmup, and hardly prepares your body for an hour-long workout the next time around. The hour session, rather than being twice as valuable as a "mere" thirty-minute workout, may actually be twice as dangerous, since it forces your body to undergo unaccustomed stress with little preparation for a period of time that is too long for a beginning exerciser. And when you finally get around to your last session of the week, the twenty-minute workout, you've actually broken down your body rather than built it up.

Consistency in PaceWalking is vitally important. By the same token, *regularity,* doing your workouts at well-balanced intervals, is no less important. Just as inconsistent workouts can do more harm than good, so bunching your workouts together, or letting too much time go between them, can hurt rather than help your fitness efforts.

For example, the PaceWalking Maintenance Program calls for workouts every other day, approximately two hours a week in all. You could meet that two-hour requirement by doing just two workouts, one hour each, say, on Saturday and Sunday. What could be more efficient? Just two days and you've satisfied a whole week's needs. Well, life doesn't work that way. Not only have you *not* realized an aerobic effect from your two-day binge (aerobic training requires at least twenty minutes, *three* days a week, remember?), but you may have hurt yourself as well. Bodies prefer being eased into things. When they're forced to do too much, too abruptly, they rebel. And the body's way of rebelling translates into injuries. Increasing the length of your workouts should be done gradually, not in one leap.

Moreover, muscles that are worked on a regular basis, at least once every other day, go though a gradual cycle of breakdown and buildup. It's two steps forward and one step back, two steps forward and one back, until finally the steps forward far outdo the steps back, and you notice increased vigor and health. But muscles that are worked only intermittently will do little but hurt after those occasional workouts and will not develop increased strength and endurance. In that case, it's one step back and no steps forward; often you may require the entire week just to recover from the damage you did. And, by the time the next weekend rolls around, you're actually in no better shape, if not in worse shape, than you were when you began.

No wonder, then, that so many weekend athletes profess little joy in their workouts. Exercising *hurts* when you only do it once in a while. And it can turn into a vicious cycle: The less you exercise, the more it hurts, so the less you exercise . . . and so on and so on. It's important that you follow fairly closely the distribution of workouts recommended in the programs to follow. They will save you a great deal of pain, lost time, and wasted effort. They will help make your PaceWalking fun *and* beneficial. Consistency and regularity—these are the passwords for aerobic health.

Pace in PaceWalking

An important key to successful PaceWalking is pace. And pace can mean a number of things.

The most obvious, of course, is your heart's pace as it does its aerobic work. Another is the pace at which you do your workouts. In PaceWalking, that pace need only be fast enough to push your heart rate into the aerobic range. It simply doesn't matter how fast you PaceWalk as long as your heart is beating between 70 and 85 percent of its maximum rate.

Pace also refers to setting a year-round exercise schedule that works for you. Eventually, you must set your own pace yourself. No one can do it for you. Guides such as this book can help, especially when you're just starting, but when it comes down to it, you're the only person who knows what you need and what you want. That's why setting reasonable goals is so important.

In PaceWalking, *you* control the training; you don't let it control you. For most of us, exercise training, no matter what it is, should not be the be-all and end-all of our lives. No workout regimen, no matter how rigorous, should disrupt your work or break up your home. In PaceWalking, if you establish reasonable goals, design your training program accordingly, and stick to it regularly and consistently, you'll almost invariably meet those goals—and, at the same time, the whole of your life will remain in balance.

Minutes, Not Miles

This may be one of the most appealing aspects of PaceWalking: *It's not how far you go but how long.* Since the primary goal of most PaceWalkers is to improve health and fitness through aerobic exercise, the key is to push your heart rate into the aerobic range for at least twenty minutes, three times a week. But whether you go two miles during those twenty minutes or half a mile, whether you walk twenty times around the block or just once, what counts is your increased heart rate and how long you sustain it.

In fact, you may now walk five miles every day, but if you don't raise your heart rate suitably, the exercise is of no aerobic help to you. A long, leisurely walk may afford you other benefits—relaxation, help in losing weight, improved flexibility, perhaps even improved strength—but aerobic benefits require aerobic exercise. Similarly, if you PaceWalk very quickly—covering a mile in under twelve minutes, for example, and pushing your heart rate well into the aerobic range—and then simply stop, you won't gain lasting aerobic benefits. Even if you walk your twelve-minute mile four times a week, even five times, you'll derive little aerobic benefit for your efforts. Twelve minutes simply isn't long enough. Distance is immaterial; what counts is time spent.

When you think about it, it's wonderfully liberating. You don't have to set yourself distance goals and then feel guilty if you don't meet them. So what if you can't—or don't want to—walk five miles, as your neighbor does or as the exercise books tell you to? And so what if you can't traverse that distance in a certain amount of time? Thinking in terms of distance gets you to thinking in terms of speed. And thinking in terms of speed can lead to frustration if, as is likely, you come to the point where you simply can't go any faster—the body *does* have its limitations, you know. And trying to push beyond those limitations often leads to injury—and pain.

PaceWalking frees you from all that. The only speed that is important for the PaceWalker is how fast your heart beats. How fast you have to walk to push your heart into the aerobic range, and how that speed compares to anyone else's speed, or to some absolute standard, is beside the point. (Of course you may want to push for speed, to measure yourself against others, or against your own best times; that can be fun as well as a good motivator. But it's important to realize that it's not necessary. Worry about speed and distance if you want to, but you can get a perfectly good workout without being concerned with either.)

Measuring your workouts in minutes and not miles also has practical advantages. You don't have to lay out specific, measured routes. You may find a favorite route that you do over and over, but that may be for pleasure, not necessity. I have one that I have done literally hundreds of times. I know how long it will take me to cover it; I don't know its length and I have no intention of ever finding out. Going by time and not by distance, you can set your pace and course according to the particular day, what the weather is like, and how you feel. A cool day may induce you to PaceWalk more quickly than usual, a hot day more slowly. It doesn't matter as long as you keep your heart rate up for the prescribed amount of time. All you need is a wristwatch, and you're off. The entire world is your training ground.

CHAPTER 3

How to PaceWalk

The PaceWalking Gait

*W*hen you get right down to it, all you're really doing in PaceWalking is *walking*. There are kinds of walking that do demand strict adherence to form. For example, race walking stipulates that the knee be locked for at least an instant when the leg is perpendicular to the ground. And it requires the heel of the forward foot to be in contact with the ground before the toe of the rear one leaves the ground. In contrast to running, during which you can be completely airborne, race walking requires that one foot be on the ground at all times; that accounts in part for the characteristic hip swinging of race walkers. In PaceWalking, you simply do what comes naturally: walk.

Your stride length should be a comfortable one. At the beginning you will probably find that, in order to get your speed up, your stride will become longer than when you walk regularly. After a while, you may find yourself shortening the length and increasing the stride rate; that's the best way to pick up speed. You may also find it comfortable to bend forward slightly while PaceWalking. If you do, bend from the hips, not the waist. Bending from the waist cramps your diaphragm and hinders your breathing.

Later on, as you become used to PaceWalking, you may want to refine your gait. For example, imagine straddling an imaginary white line while you PaceWalk and try to step onto the line with each stride; your gait will be smoother and more efficient. Ideally, the heel of your forward foot should land directly in front of the big toe of the trailing foot, Indian fashion. But this gait takes some practice, and some balance. If it doesn't come naturally or easily at the beginning, don't worry about it.

In PaceWalking, unlike running, arm motion is as important as leg motion. Why? Because without a determined and constant swing of the arms, most people find it impossible to walk fast enough to move their heart rate into the aerobic range. If you haven't been doing any exercise at all, you'll find walking just a little more quickly than usual will raise your heart rate. But after a few weeks of that kind of walking, your body will adapt, your heart will slow back down to a lower rate, and you'll no longer realize an aerobic effect. If PaceWalking is to become your way of doing aerobic exercise, you must incorporate a vigorous arm swing into your gait.

Here's how. Swing your arms back and forth, along the same plane as your forward movement. Your fingers should be lightly closed, *not* clenched. Clenched fingers are one of the surest signs of tension—not a good idea when doing any kind of exercise. The idea is to stay relaxed. Your arms should be comfortably bent, at about a 90-degree angle. On the forward swing, your hand should reach a comfortable level above your waist. Then swing back and stop when you feel the muscles on the back part of your shoulder begin to stretch.

Don't swing your arms across your chest. Such an oblique motion can provide a vigorous arm swing, true, but it hinders your forward momentum. The twisting motion it sets up in your torso can also lead to injury. Keep your arms swinging generally front to back, not side to side, and while the swing should be vigorous, it should not be overly so. You want to avoid tension, muscle clenching, and tightness in your arms and shoulders.

Refining the Gait Further

It is important not to get hung up on the technical details of the gait if you find such things boring or hindering. What is impor-

Correct PaceWalking gait and arm swing

How *not* to swing your arms while PaceWalking

tant about PaceWalking is to have fun and to get your heart rate up into the aerobic range. But if you are interested in developing a smooth, flowing, faster gait, there are a few things you can do. They take some practice and concentration, but you may find the extra effort worth it.

Try to keep your spine straight. Don't be rigid about it, but do adopt a relaxed, upright posture. Keep your head level. If you must look down at the pavement immediately in front of you, don't bend your neck, but rather, cast your eyes downward. Don't scrunch up your shoulders to achieve that straight spine, however. Try to keep them loose, dropped, and relaxed.

For the footstrike, come down first on the outside corner of your heel, then roll forward along the outside edge of your foot, pushing off with all your toes at the same time. Some people like to visualize grabbing the ground with their toes as they push off. But don't curl your toes and end up cramping them.

Keep your hips nice and loose. You can roll them gently from side to side if you wish to, as a race walker does. But the true race-walking hip roll is a complex rotation that takes practice to perfect. Don't worry about it, and don't worry about heel-toe movement, when to straighten your leg, and so on. If you would like to race walk as well as PaceWalk, it would be a good idea to enroll in a class or take some individual lessons. It's hard to learn race walking on your own. It's very easy to learn PaceWalking on your own.

The Aerobic Gait

It's the combination of leg stride and arm swing, however you do them, that makes PaceWalking an aerobic exercise for most people. And that provides PaceWalking with one of the advantages it has over most other major aerobic activities. Unlike swimming, biking, and running, PaceWalking provides a good workout for *two* of the major muscle groups—arms and legs—not just one. Rowing and cross-country skiing also provide such a two-faceted workout, but they're not nearly as popular, they require much more equipment and training, and, of course, they must have special weather conditions and special locales. Of the remaining popular aerobic activities, only aerobic dance works more than one major muscle group.

So, step smartly and swing smartly—the two ingredients of PaceWalking. Try to develop a nice, smooth, regular rhythm. Any extraneous movement will only waste energy and tire you out. A head that bobs up and down, a torso that bends forward at the waist and twists this way and that—these unnecessary motions detract from the efficiency of your PaceWalk.

But don't sweat the details. For beginning PaceWalkers especially, the point is to get out and get moving, drive your heart rate into the aerobic range, and enjoy yourself. Relax and do what comes naturally. If that means some leaning forward, some head bobbing and torso twisting, so be it. As long as you're enjoying your workout, benefiting from it, and not injuring yourself (injuries are another possible, and even less welcome, by-product of extraneous movement)—you're doing okay. If you want to become smoother, more graceful, more relaxed, and more efficient, you can learn that later on. And many people find that if they just PaceWalk enough, without even thinking about it they will begin to smooth out and speed up.

Rhythmic Breathing

Breathing *is* something that may be worth worrying about. In the beginning, you'll probably find you're not breathing hard. But as your stamina and proficiency increase, and you begin to walk faster, your rate of breathing will increase. And since the whole idea of aerobic exercise is to utilize more efficiently breathed-in air, it's a good idea to breathe as efficiently as possible.

That means deep, rhythmic breaths, pulling the air deep into your lungs. Efficient breathing involves the diaphragm, which expands the lungs downward, and the chest muscles, which expand the rib cage, and therefore the lungs, outward. Breathe the air *down*, toward the stomach. Move your abdomen outwards. Short, high chest breaths are simply not as useful; you'll find yourself out of breath much more easily if you only breathe into the top part of your lungs. Imagine the air filling your lungs as water fills an empty barrel, from the bottom up.

As your speed and rate of breathing pick up, you might find it most comfortable to link your breathing with your gait. For example, you might breathe in for three paces, then breathe out for three paces, and so on. Or in for two, out for two; in for four, out for four. Find the pace that's good for you. Rhythmic breathing can help establish the overall rhythm, smoothness, and balance that make PaceWalking so pleasurable.

If you get tired, one trick is to abandon the rhythmic pattern for a few cycles and forcibly blow out the air for a count longer than that of breathing in. For example, breathe in for three paces, breathe out for three, then force out all the remaining air on step four. Breathing this way often provides a quick renewal of energy. No one is certain just why it works, but it does. It may have something to do with clearing all the stale air out of the alveoli, the little breathing sacs in the lungs through which oxygen is transferred from the air into your blood.

Some people get "stitches" while PaceWalking. The pain of a stitch is usually due to cramping of the diaphragm, but there are several possible causes. You can get the quickest relief by pressing hard with three fingers on the point where the pain is concentrated, usually just under the rib cage, while exhaling forcefully. You can even do this while continuing to PaceWalk.

Measurements

How to Determine Your Aerobic Heart Rate

The whole business of determining your aerobic heart rate can be reduced to a simple formula. First, subtract your age from 220;

the result is your theoretical maximum heart rate. Now take 70 percent of that number; that's the minimum rate you want to sustain for at least twenty minutes of your workout. (For safety reasons, you should not go above 85 percent of your maximum heart rate.)

For example, if you're forty years old, your maximum heart rate is 220 minus 40—that's 180 beats per minute, right? And 70 to 85 percent of 180 is 126 to 153 beats per minute. If you can keep your heart rate above 126 beats per minute for twenty minutes, you're in business. That pace, done at least three times a week, will give you aerobic benefits. A sixty-year-old needs a heart rate of at least 112 beats per minute, a twenty-year-old at least 140 beats.

Minimum Aerobic Heart Rates for Selected Ages

Age	Heart Rate
21	139
25	136
30	133
35	130
39	127
40	126
45	123
50	119
55	116
60	112
65	109
70	105
75	102
80	98
85	95
90	91

Based on 70 percent of 220 minus age.

How to Measure Your Heart Rate

To measure your heart rate you have to find your pulse, but you need not assume the classic pose of a doctor grasping the patient's wrist. There's a much easier way to do it. If you run your finger down your neck on either side from just below your ear to the middle of your collarbone, you'll find a thick band of muscle. Feel it? Now just in front of that muscle, toward your Adam's apple, is a groove. If you hold your index and middle fingers together and gently press them into that groove, you'll feel the pulsing of your carotid artery. That's the artery that supplies blood to the head and neck. The pulse rate there is the same as the pulse rate at your wrist.

How to measure your pulse

Caution: *Do not press on both sides of your neck at the same time.* You could cause yourself to pass out, or worse. Taking your pulse on just one side of your neck is perfectly safe, unless you have carotid artery disease in one or both arteries. Symptoms of carotid artery disease include brief, temporary paralysis of one or more muscle groups; temporary changes in skin sensation, such as numbness and tingling, and visual disturbances, such as double vision, headache, dizziness, and light-headedness. These symptoms are sometimes accompanied by a noise or vibration in the neck coming from the carotid artery. If you have any of these symptoms, check with your doctor before taking your pulse in this manner.

Now that you know how to take your pulse, count the beats for ten seconds, then multiply by six, or count the beats for six seconds and multiply by ten. Twenty beats during a ten-second interval translates to 120 beats per minute—right on the money for a fifty-year-old.

But if all this higher math and advanced physiology puts you off, there's a quick and dirty way of determining the same thing. Approach your PaceWalking with the idea that you want to break a sweat but be able to carry on a conversation. The perspiration ensures that you've probably worked hard enough to move your heart rate into the aerobic range; the conversation indicates that you haven't worked so hard that you're out of breath.

For many people, to begin with at least, all it takes to get the heart rate up is to walk slightly faster than normal. The ideal PaceWalking workout for many people might well result in a sheen of perspiration on the forehead and a stimulating discussion with your partner—double benefits. Thus one of the attractions of PaceWalking: It's so *civilized*.

Where to PaceWalk

You're primed and ready to go. Now the question is, *where?*

With PaceWalking, it's not much of a question—not compared to other activities, anyway. You don't have to find a track, or a pool, or a studio, or a parcourse, or a gym, or a court. In fact, you don't have to find anything. Just open your front door and go. And because time, not distance, is the point of PaceWalking, you don't need to hunt out a suitably distant destination. You can get in a good PaceWalking workout by doing no more than circling the block a few times, if it comes to that.

Of course, there may be more enjoyable things to do than circle the block. And some routes are safer than others, whether because of physical situations or human conditions. So here are some hints on how to pick the very best PaceWalking routes for yourself.

Parks

In general, the best places to PaceWalk are parks. Especially so if the parks have certain paths or roadways set aside expressly for walkers, runners, and, if there's room, cyclists. Central Park in Manhattan is a good example. Special paths mean a continuous stretch of pavement *with no motor traffic*. What a pleasure. And they mean company as well, for parks with provisions for exercisers attract such people. It can be reassuring, as well as fun, to exercise with other exercisers around, especially in city parks.

And parks mean pleasant surroundings. Often there will be hills, usually not too steep, that present a challenge and welcome variety. And the presence of trees, grass, lakes, ponds, and streams is a tonic. Many people view their time spent PaceWalking through these surroundings as the highlight of their day. Others consider it a necessary transition that helps them resolve what the day has dealt them so far and prepares them to handle what may come later on.

And, if nothing else, PaceWalking through such a setting offers an ideal opportunity to think. It's a private time—your own—for many people the only personal moment in their entire day. It's true that you can accomplish a perfectly good aerobic workout by PaceWalking along busy streets. (You must deal with having to inhale exhaust fumes, though. Polluted air, whether from automobiles or industry, is a fact of life for most city dwellers. It's hard to escape pollution, but parks may offer a partial respite.) But the mind and spirit do better in pleasant surroundings. If at all possible, head for the park.

Countryside

Country roads and lanes often offer a pleasant setting for PaceWalking, assuming the walking surface is good. Dirt roads are the least attractive, since they're often rough, uneven, or strewn with rocks; to avoid injury, you have to concentrate on the road surface rather than on your PaceWalking. Concrete pavement is the next best bet because it offers a smooth, consistent surface; but concrete is hard and unyielding. Better that you should PaceWalk on blacktop if at all possible. Blacktop is softer than concrete and offers some resilience. Today's shoes are built for use on blacktop. A good pair of shoes and a good blacktop surface might make your legs think they're walking on the grass.

Suburbs

Lightly trafficked streets in suburban neighborhoods are often good for PaceWalking. The pavement is usually smooth and of blacktop. Suburbs also often offer the possibility of working out on nearby school running tracks, possibly the best surfaces of all. Most schools make their tracks available for public use except during after-school practice hours. The only problem with PaceWalking on a track is boredom. But boredom can be alleviated by working out with a partner—of either the two- or four-footed variety.

Cities

Living in a city neighborhood that does not have ready access to a park with a suitable walking path can present problems for the

PaceWalker. They can be overcome, of course, and city dwellers do overcome them all the time, but you must be very attentive to your surroundings, the condition of the pavement, traffic, other pedestrians, traffic signals—all of which take your mind off your goal, which is to get a good aerobic workout. But for many of us, there's no other choice. And faced with having to navigate city streets or give up your workout, it's worth exploring the city streets.

Walk on the sidewalk, if at all possible. If you have to walk in the street, do so against the traffic. Try to find a time of day that's less congested than other times. And be *careful*. Working out is great, but staying healthy and in one piece is greater.

Malls

A relatively new setting for PaceWalking are the many enclosed shopping malls springing up around the country. And when you think about it, why not? The malls protect walkers from weather that's unsuitable at either end of the thermometer. They offer a constant temperature of 68 to 70 degrees, they're well lit and relatively safe all day long, and when you're done, what could be easier than to duck into a nearby shop or restaurant as a reward for your efforts?

Some shopping malls even encourage walkers by offering a series of exercise stations along a measured walking trail. Since mallwalking often attracts senior citizens, some malls offer weekly blood-pressure tests and booths where walkers can check their coats, sign in, and log their walks. In Boulder, Colorado, Crossroads Mall and Boulder Memorial Hospital have teamed up to form a mallwalking club, complete with walking charts that allow participants to Walk the Orient, or Walk Alaska to Acapulco. More than one hundred mallwalkers have completed a Walk Across America, that proclaimed each mile of mallwalking equal to 25 freeway miles. These hardy souls trekked the 2,925 miles between Los Angeles and Washington, D.C., in 117 mall miles. Mallwalking offers good exercise, good company, and travel by shorthand—that is, short *foot*.

Some Favorite Places

Some of my favorite places to PaceWalk are as follows:

• Central Park in Manhattan is a wonderful place to exercise. You can do the 1.6-mile loop around the reservoir located in the northern half of the park, or you can walk 4 to 6 miles along the park drives (which are closed to vehicles at all times except weekday rush hours). And you'll have lots of company, most of it good.

• Prospect Park in Brooklyn, New York, has a lovely 3.4-mile loop of park drive that is reserved for walkers, runners, and cyclists during most daylight hours of the week. As in Central Park, though, stay alert. It's all too easy to suddenly be overtaken by a bicycler in a hurry. A hint: Hold your ground; don't make any sudden moves in one direction or another. These bicyclers have a finely developed sense of distance. They'll pass you with a hair to spare.

• Boston's Charles River offers beautiful pathways for several miles along both sides of this picturesque waterway. The Fens also offer lovely walking territory.

• In Philadelphia there is a beautiful boulevard called The Parkway, which leads from the business district to the Museum of Art (where you can PaceWalk up the steps with the *Rocky* theme playing in your head), and then past it to a pleasant path along the Schuylkill River.

• Chicago's Lake Front is a magnificent place to PaceWalk. Lake Shore Drive runs for several miles through a fine park along Lake Michigan from The Loop at the center of the city north along the Gold Coast and south to the Museum of Science and Industry. There are beautiful views of both the city and the lake.

• Washington, D.C., offers many miles of flat paths with fine vistas of the Potomac River, national monuments, elegant government buildings, and parklands. A favorite route for many people is around the Mall—from the Capitol, past the Smithsonian Institution museums, between the Washington Monument and the White House, along the Reflecting Pool, to the Vietnam and Lincoln memorials and back. A moving as well as exhilarating PaceWalk. Also in Washington is a most enjoyable path through Rock Creek Park, which runs northeast from the River Road along the District side of the Potomac, just a few blocks north of the Kennedy Center.

• The Trinity Trail, which runs for miles along the banks of the Trinity River in Forth Worth, Texas, is quiet and smooth, has no vehicular traffic, and is for walkers, runners, and cyclists only. It's great for PaceWalking.

• In Denver, try Washington Park. It offers a 2.2-mile asphalt loop that is closed to all vehiclar traffic. It's a favorite route for walkers, cyclists, and runners alike. The park itself is grassy, filled with trees—maple, fir, pine—and dotted with flowers of all kinds. And pervading all is that gorgeous Colorado blue sky and thin crisp air. There are times, especially in fall and spring, when it's easy to think that this must be paradise. Washington Park also offers a recreation center complete with weights and an olympic-size swimming pool.

• In San Francisco, you can park at the marina and then PaceWalk along the bay almost to the base of the Golden Gate Bridge and back. It's a 3-mile round trip, complete with lapping waves, screeching gulls, and, when the fog allows, a magnificent view of the bridge and Alcatraz. And afterward you can wander through the marina and enjoy its endless variety of sailboats.

• In Hawaii, as you might expect, there are many beautiful walks with great scenery. A favorite of mine is the road east from Waikiki, Honolulu, through Kapiolani Park and then on up and down the road that winds around the base of Diamond Head. Ocean on one side and one of the most famous mountains in the world on the other. Pretty hard to beat.

Finding Places to PaceWalk

You may already have your own places in mind, even though you haven't yet used them for PaceWalking. If not, you might contact a walking or running club in your area for some suggestions.(See appendix for a list of clubs and other suggestions.)

Many city and county governments have departments of parks or recreation that can provide you with information on places to PaceWalk. You can usually get hold of them through the local telephone directory. States have departments of parks and recreation, as well. Their offices are usually in the state capital; you can write or call for information (see appendix 3). And on the national level, contact:

> THE NATIONAL PARK SERVICE
> Public Inquiries
> P.O. Box 37127
> Washington, D.C. 20013–7127

They provide information about national parks, national monuments, and related areas. You can find many opportunities for PaceWalking when vacationing in these spots.

When to PaceWalk

When should you PaceWalk? Whenever it is best for you. Everyone differs in this regard. Dr. Kenneth Cooper, who has done so much to spread the aerobics message around the world, thinks that working out just before dinner is best. His reason is that exercise promotes the secretion of the hormone insulin, which mobilizes energy-supplying glycogen from the liver, making you feel less hungry. Therefore, you'll eat less at dinner—for many of us, a blessing.

Many people like to work out in the morning, before breakfast. I count myself in that number. Morning workouts can give you a psychological lift that lasts the entire day. If your workplace has showers and locker facilities, a lunchtime workout might be the ticket. It certainly provides a break and a change of scene that can be very therapeutic. The rest of the workday can look much brighter after a good workout.

But, unless you have no other choice, it's usually not a good idea to PaceWalk at night. Many parks are not safe at night, even if there are other exercisers around. As for unlit roads, even if you wear a reflective vest or clothing and always walk facing traffic, you run a much higher risk of injury, either from tripping or falling, or being hit by a vehicle, than you do during the day. If you must exercise outdoors at night, stick to well-lit streets or roads in neighborhoods you know to be safe.

Other Safety Hints

Be Aware

It's true that one of the great pleasures of aerobic exercise is the opportunity to get away, alone with your thoughts. For many people, it's the only time to be alone, truly alone. Sometimes very creative things happen during these times. Other times very peaceful, calming things occur. Some exercisers report getting so far into another world that they forget where they are and what they are doing. That's all well and good, but unless you're working out in an especially isolated place, losing yourself can be dangerous.

It's important always to maintain some level of awareness of your surroundings. You don't want to have a collision with another PaceWalker, runner, or pedestrian. You don't want to be hit by a car or bicycle. You don't want to be caught completely unaware by an animal or a human predator.

So indulge yourself in your privacy. Do think those good

thoughts. But at the same time keep a weather eye out for trouble. Try to anticipate problems and avoid them if at all possible.

Be Defensive

If you suspect, or have heard, that your PaceWalking route might be dangerous, prepare in advance to defend yourself. Here are a few suggestions as to how to do that:

• A whistle can be very useful for warning cars or cyclists that you're in the vicinity. It also can scare off both two- and four-footed attackers.

• Don't carry anything valuable. Your office or club locker or your own home is the place for your wallet or purse. If you bring along a couple of dollars to buy a newspaper and cup of coffee at the end of your PaceWalk, and somebody demands them, hand them over. In general, give no one the idea that you're harboring anything worth taking. The only valuable thing on the PaceWalking path should be yourself.

• Plan ahead. Don't use paths in a park that you know are especially risky. Have some idea of how you might make an escape if trouble looms ahead. Don't PaceWalk on paths that have many obstacles. For example, some hiking trails have boulders, ruts, or large tree roots across them. Others are covered with leaves, and can be slippery. Dirt paths can turn to quagmires when it rains or snows. And it is a very good idea to wear an identification tag so that in the case of really serious trouble, police or medical personnel will know who you are and where to call in an emergency.

Keep Your Head Up

Many of us have a tendency to look squarely at the ground just ahead of our feet while we PaceWalk, and sometimes it's necessary to do so to avoid potholes or unexpected bumps and crevices. But look ahead as well. Some problems come from above or ahead: an overhanging branch, a fallen power line, a potentially dangerous dog, a suspicious-looking person. Keeping your head up ensures that you're able to see erratically moving cars, or cars that are backing out of driveways or turning onto the road in your direction. You'll see cyclists, runners, and other PaceWalkers. You'll have an idea of how far you've gone and how far you must go to return home.

And keeping your head up provides more subtle, psychological returns as well. There's something about looking up and out that elevates and expands the spirit, whereas looking at your feet can signify a depressed state of mind. Look up and ahead; see where you are going. Be aware of possibilities and make plans to meet them—that's the PaceWalking mentality.

Think Twice About Headphones

This is a tough one. Headphones are great, no doubt about it. There's nothing quite like listening to music with phones on. It makes you feel as though you're *inside* the music, as though it's emanating from your own head. Headphones block out the world. But they are not such a good idea when it comes to PaceWalking. Blocking out the world is the last thing you want to do while exercising in a public place or in a potentially dangerous situation.

But, you might argue, even if I'm listening to headphones, I can *see* where I'm going. I can *see* potential problems. True enough. But in some situations, seeing is not enough. How often do we *hear* approaching automobiles, for example, before we see them? Or hear the footsteps of an approaching runner or the warning bell of an approaching bicyclist? As far as I'm concerned, headphones just aren't worth the risk.

But all is not lost. If you must have music, put the earphones on *in front* of your ears. Your skull will transmit the music inside your head while your ears will still be open to outside sounds. Just don't play the music too loudly. Or try one of those vests equipped with speakers. The sound is almost as good, the effect of being surrounded by music almost as strong.

Equipment for PaceWalking

I'd like to go on record right now. If you want to buy lots of neat stuff to do your PaceWalking in, bravo! Enjoy. But don't think you have to. In fact, except for comfort *vis-à-vis* the weather, there's only one pressing concern—shoes.

Shoes

Good shoes for PaceWalking have two necessary ingredients: a firm heel and a flexible forefoot.

First, the forefoot. When you're PaceWalking, the front part of your foot bends a great deal. Try walking across the room and you'll see. Your shoe must be able to *bend* with your foot but not *bind* it. And the shoe shouldn't press into the top of your foot when its flexed. You should know the shoe is there, but it should allow your foot all the flexibility it needs to walk briskly.

Second, the heel should be firm and provide good support. Your foot should feel that it is firmly *in* the shoe, not simply *on* it. And because the pressure of the downstroke of the walking gait is so much less than that of running, the heavy heel cushioning found in many running shoes is not necessary in PaceWalking shoes.

Remember that a shoe that feels particularly soft in the beginning may prove to be much too soft when you wear it over and over. If in doubt, start with an overly firm shoe rather than the other way around.

A few more hints:

Although there are many sizes of shoes, there are even more sizes of feet. If your foot is one of those that just doesn't conform to the shoemaker's categories, fit your foot to the forefoot of the shoe,

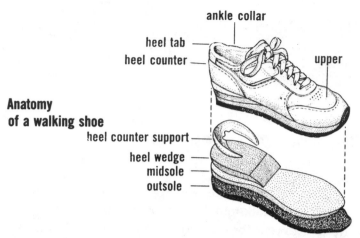

ankle collar

heel tab

heel counter

upper

**Anatomy
of a walking shoe**

heel counter support

heel wedge

midsole

outsole

not to the heel. You can always firm up the heel by using a heel insert, but if your foot is uncomfortable in the shoe's forefoot, whether too tight or too loose, you're out of luck.

Although the shoe certainly should not feel tight, it should be in complete contact with your foot. You don't want your foot moving around inside the shoe. You can take up any slack in an overly large shoe by adding an extra inner sole or by wearing a thick pair of socks. But if the shoe is too *small*, you're in trouble.

Fit the shoe in the store. Don't expect it to stretch to your foot. It used to be that people bought shoes a little tight so that when the shoes stretched they'd be just right. No longer. The materials used in the most modern sports shoes don't give much. If your walking shoes don't feel right in the shop, it's highly unlikely that they will ever feel right.

Walk around in the shoes before buying them. Shoes that may feel okay while you're standing there admiring them in the mirror may *not* feel okay once you start walking in them. And if your store allows it, take a good, brisk PaceWalk in the new shoes outside on the pavement.

It's a good idea to buy at least your first pair of walking shoes from a shop that specializes in walking or running shoes. Later on you may want to shop at a discount store or a mail-order house. But at first let the people in the specialty shop help you find the right shoes. Most of these people walk or run themselves, and they are able to give you good advice as to the proper fit and the characteristics of the various shoes they sell, as well as share experiences that others have had with various models and brands. Then, for your next pair, you'll have a stronger sense of what you need as well as what you want.

Although there are many brands and models of shoes, there are few real differences in quality between one and another in the same general price range. Most of the differences are cosmetic or have to do with how a certain design fits your particular foot. It may be that a number of shoes will meet your comfort requirements; after that, it's just a matter of style and price. And no one can make those judgments but you.

Clothing

Clothing should be loose-fitting and comfortable—cool enough in warm weather, warm enough in cool weather. And that's just about it.

The "cool enough in warm weather" business offers little difficulty. But it may be tough, oddly enough, to stay cool enough in cool weather because it's easy to overdress at the beginning. It's no fun having to lug around a heavy winter coat during your workout, either on your back or on your arm.

On cool days, dress so that you feel just a little on the chilly side at the beginning. If you feel nice and toasty, you're almost certain to become hot and uncomfortable well before the end. No matter how cold it is, once you get going you'll begin to perspire; that's part of the plan. If you're wearing heavy sweats, however, all that moisture will stay right where it is—that is, condensed on your skin. So for cold-weather PaceWalking, several layers of light- to moderate-weight garments are much better than one heavyweight set. If your Windbreaker or sweater becomes too warm during your PaceWalk, it's easy enough to take it off, tie it around your shoulders or waist, and continue your workout. And, above all, wear clothing that can breathe, either through the fabric or through vents in the garment.

The best materials to wear next to your skin are artificial fibers, such as polypropylene, that transport moisture from their warmer side, next to the skin, to their cooler side, away from the skin. That means that the perspiration generated from exercise can evaporate much more easily than it can when trapped next to the skin by a heavy cotton sweat suit.

Good outer layers include synthetic fabrics with billions of tiny pores that let perspiration moisture out and won't let wind or rain drops in. That and a warm hat and gloves can make PaceWalking in the wintertime a delightful experience.

Five quick hints:

- Wear socks. They help avoid blisters.
- Take along a lightweight nylon backpack to house any number of clothing mistakes.
- Women should wear a jogging bra.
- Men should wear support briefs or an athletic supporter.
- Mount a thermometer outside your bedroom window.

Stopwatch

It doesn't have to be fancy; all you need is a watch to time the duration of your workout and check your heart rate. Some people still like the old-fashioned hand-held variety, which you can set at the beginning of your PaceWalk, slip into your pocket, pull out to check your heart rate, and then put away again until the end of your workout. They're still around, and they don't have to cost very much—from about $20 and up.

But most people now use digital watches. As everyone knows, there is a wide variety that do just about any task you can think of. A little more than $15 will buy you all you need for PaceWalking. The prime consideration is that the watch be easy to set and easy to read. And although you don't need a watch that's waterproof to 300 feet, some waterproofing, say to 50 feet, is a nice feature. Then you won't have to worry should you get caught in the rain or if you go out in the rain on purpose. And PaceWalking in a light rain on a warm summer's day can be an absolutely delightful experience.

How to Make PaceWalking Fun

For some people it doesn't matter much whether an experience is pleasurable or not. What counts are the results. In fact, often PaceWalkers are asked, "Isn't it boring?" Well, yes, it can be. But when you realize that as a result of this "boring" activity you feel better and look better, with more energy and a clearer mind, and you have a reduced risk of a wide variety of diseases, it's awfully easy to put up with a couple of hours of "boredom" every week.

But that's not the PaceWalking philosophy. I feel that although every day may not be an absolutely delightful experience, Pace-Walkers should approach their workout with the anticipation that it might be. And more than that, they should devise ways of ensuring that, if nothing else, it won't be boring.

Here are some suggestions as to how to make PaceWalking fun.

The Sport Is Intrinsically Enjoyable

Everyone has experienced the pleasure of a good walk. PaceWalking is that and more. It's a smooth, flowing activity. You move rhythmically and breathe rhythmically. It can be exhilarating to be in control of your body, to make it do things it hasn't done before. With the right arm swing you can produce a heady sensation of speed—you really glide along.

Combine that intrinsic enjoyment with the pleasure of being outdoors, and the experience is even more satisfying. When you're dressed properly, a PaceWalk on a sunny, cold, crisp day can be marvelously invigorating. A light rain can increase the pleasure. The summertime is great for those who like to work up a hefty sweat (and a PaceWalker can go longer in hotter weather than just about any other exerciser). The very best times of year for most people are spring and fall, when the sun is shining and the temperature is just right. PaceWalking can connect you with the environment more intimately than any other exercise activity.

Use PaceWalking as a Time for Thinking

You can plan your day if you work out in the morning, or review it if you exercise in the evening. PaceWalking can be a particularly productive time (I did a great deal of conceptualizing for this book while PaceWalking) or a relaxing one. If you have personal problems to deal with, there's no better time. No phone, no doorbell, no interruptions from family, friends, or office-mates. Just you alone with your thoughts. It's your time. Make the most of it.

Change Your Routes

Some PaceWalkers enjoy doing the same route over and over again. I fall into that category. I have a route that takes me fifty-five to sixty minutes to cover, through lightly traveled streets in my neighborhood and along a beautiful stretch of harbor. It has the right combination of uphill, flat, and downhill—I like it. I do it over and over again.

But other people like variety. You can learn several different routes in your neighborhood, each with different challenges. Or it may be time to explore new territory, even if it requires driving to a starting off point away from your usual neck of the woods. Whatever the mechanics of getting there, a change of scene is one of the foolproof ways of averting boredom.

Set Nonexercise-Related Goals

Add an errand to your workout. Plan to pick up the morning newspaper, or a carton of milk, or a loaf of bread. PaceWalk to the post office and back, or the bank, or the library (here's where a lightweight nylon backpack can be especially handy). If your car needs servicing, you might drive to the garage, leave the car, and PaceWalk home. Then reverse the procedure when the vehicle is ready.

To complement this approach, you can give yourself nonexercise-related rewards. A special meal, a new movie or tape, some clothing you've been wanting, a new book, a night on the town—anything to make the PaceWalking a means to an end outside itself.

Be Ingenious

Try using a walking stick, for example. First, it may make you feel like a real walker; second, it may help you develop a good PaceWalking rhythm. You can use it to count lampposts or utility poles. You can twirl it like a baton. You can raise it high as though you were a drum major. You can drag it in the dust behind you or forcibly plunk it down on the pavement ahead of you—the possibilities are numerous. Use your imagination to give your PaceWalk life and surprise.

Keep a PaceWalking Diary

A diary of your workouts can be helpful for dealing with boredom, as well as getting you to maintain the consistency and regularity in training that I stress so much. You can use a little spiral notebook, or buy one of the many diaries designed especially for keeping track of exercise programs.

The form and format don't matter; the content does. For each workout, record the date, time, scheduled number of minutes, how long you actually PaceWalked, what the course and the weather were like, how you felt, how some new piece of equipment or combination of clothing worked on that particular day, any special thoughts you might have had, and so on. Such a diary helps to locate each workout in a continuum of others—it becomes part of a larger sequence—and so you can easily compare one workout to another, recall especially good or bad ones, and plan ahead to others. That makes things more fun.

PaceWalk with a Companion

It's the most common advice you'll hear with respect to just about any exercise activity. And it's true. There's nothing like good conversation, or even not-so-good conversation, to make a workout session fly by. The problem is finding a suitable partner. You need someone with whom you can establish a common schedule. You need someone who works out at about your pace. (Actually, it's best to have a partner who likes to go slightly faster than you do; it stretches you a bit. But that's not so good for your partner.) And this person should be someone you like and can talk with easily.

A tough combination of attributes. It may be that the best you can do is find someone to exercise with on occasion. Even that may be better than nothing.

There is one type of companion who satisfies most of these requirements, however, and is often extremely loyal, affectionate, and dependable, besides. That's a four-footed friend. There are many advantages to working out with your dog. You don't have to talk when you don't want to, and you don't have to adjust to anyone's schedule but your own. You'll never get anything but an enthusiastic welcome when it's time to go, and you'll never out-PaceWalk your dog. And in certain neighborhoods and at certain times of day, usually very late, your dog might be a very welcome companion, especially if it weighs at least half as much as you do.

There is, of course, the problem of convincing your dog that PaceWalking and dog walking are two different things. Your dog must learn that pauses at fire hydrants and lampposts, stops to get acquainted with other dogs, and breaks to sniff out the most interesting odors in the neighborhood are better done on dog-walking time rather than while PaceWalking. Once trained, however, your dog will trot along with you, at *your* pace.

Try Racing

There may be nothing that intensifies PaceWalking quite as much as the scent of competition. Later on I devote an entire chapter to racing (see chapter 7). Suffice it to say here that any PaceWalker who can maintain a twelve- to thirteen-minute mile can certainly do a local 5- or 10-kilometer (3.1 and 6.2 miles, respectively) runner's road race and be reasonably certain of finishing before the course is closed. An increasing number of local road races now have provisions for both race walkers and PaceWalkers. But even if the race you might like to try does not have such a provision, there are usually at least a few runners out there who will be going more slowly than you over the whole course.

There are two primary reasons why you might want to try racing. First, races are just plain fun. You meet a lot of healthy, interesting people, and most of them are there to participate and complete the course, not to win. So there's very little competition, and almost everyone is there to have a good time.

Second, racing can provide a focus for your training—the frosting on the cake. And regular races also provide a series of events that break up long stretches of training into manageable pieces.

Preparing to Pacewalk

Stretching

As compared to most other exercise activities, PaceWalking demands little in the way of stretching. That may be a heretical thing to say, especially in these days of stretching classes, stretching books, and stretching TV shows. Stretching is *in*, that's clear. But just how much good stretching really does may not be quite so clear.

To begin with, why stretch at all? It's a good question, one that should be asked more often. Prevailing sentiment aside, is there any real benefit in regularly forcing your muscles and tendons (the tough cords that connect muscles to bones) to stretch?

Well, the answer is yes. Stretching may be worth doing *if*—and it's a big if—it's done for the right reasons. Stretching to prepare your body for an activity, to loosen you up after your workout, or to help rehabilitate an injury may be worth doing. Stretching for its own sake, done simply to increase your flexibility, may not be. And besides, you can hurt yourself along the way.

As recently as about twenty-five years ago, few people thought much about stretching. It was then that football players began to use weights to help get in shape. Weights meant free weights, of course: barbells and dumbbells. This was before the days of weight-training machines. So in order to use as much weight as possible, people lifted through a limited range of motion. Try it. If you want to strengthen your biceps muscles in the upper arm, for example, you can handle much more weight if you begin lifting with your arms bent at a right angle than if you begin with them straight out in front of you. The same goes for your legs and the rest of the muscles in your body.

The result of all this limited lifting was an impressive array of bulging muscles but not much flexibility. The muscles looked great, but they were tight—thus the term "muscle-bound"—and easily injured. Tight muscles tear more readily than loose muscles.

**Lifting through a
limited range of motion**

In an attempt to conteract the injuries, the lifters turned to stretching. If they could stretch out a muscle beforehand, maybe it wouldn't tighten up too much and tear so easily during lifting.

Then came the fitness boom, and what was once little more than an attempt to keep football players from injuring themselves while lifting weights became an end in itself. Flexibility for its own sake became the goal, as though there were something wrong with being relatively stiff—the fate of most of us. And as more and more people began to stretch, a funny thing happened: Sports medicine doctors began to see people who had been injured *while stretching*. The fact is that too much stretching can do more than loosen muscles and tendons; it can actually stretch ligaments—not a good idea—and injure joints.

People should be careful about stretching. As a means to an end, yes, stretching can do good things for you. As an end in itself, maybe not. So if your activity demands flexibility—gymnastics and dancing come to mind—then stretching beforehand is absolutely necessary to avoid injury. If your activity requires flexibility in a limited way—tennis players who have to rear back to serve, for example, and baseball pitchers who must wind up to throw—then stretching can help. And for the rest of us—people who jog, swim a few laps in the pool, lift a few weights, or PaceWalk—stretching can be a good thing to loosen up, to get your blood flowing and your muscles loose and help prevent soreness the next day.

Stretches for PaceWalkers

Here are a few stretches that won't do you any harm—and they will probably do some good. If nothing else, they *feel* good. You may do them as regularly as you like. If you miss a day or two, don't worry. It's the nature of PaceWalking that it doesn't require any particular preparation. I find that my workout goes better when I stretch before starting out than when I don't. On the other hand, I know people who don't stretch at all and get along fine. The important thing is that, if you do stretch, stretch slowly and gently. *Do not* bounce into stretches; bouncing can too rapidly overstretch the muscles and cause tears. It's one of the easiest ways to injure yourself. Stretch slowly, gently, holding the stretch at the point where you begin to feel it, then stretch a bit more. Remember, the idea is to loosen the muscles and tendons, to warm them, and to increase their blood supply, *not* to see how flexible you can be. Your goal is to PaceWalk more effectively, not to imitate a pretzel.

Stretch before PaceWalking *and* afterwards. Especially if you feel tight or sore, stretch afterwards. When muscles become tired they tighten up. And they tend to stay tightened up for quite a while. It's your body's way of protecting itself, of persuading you not to use those muscles again. The result is soreness, aching, pain. Stretching afterwards helps loosen the tired muscles and *keep* them loosened. That, in turn, keeps you from hurting. Even if you don't bother to stretch beforehand, it can be a good idea to stretch afterwards, especially if you're tired and sore.

Achilles Tendon and Calf Stretch

The Achilles tendon is the large cable that runs from your heel to your calf muscles; you can easily feel it between your fingers. It's

**Straight leg
Achilles tendon stretch**

**Bent leg
Achilles tendon stretch**

the largest and most exposed tendon in the body and one of the most easily injured. Achilles tendinitis is one of the most common injuries suffered by people who exercise. In walking, the Achilles tendon and calf muscles stretch every time you take a step.

To stretch the Achilles tendon, stand with your feet pointing straight in front of you, one leg in front of the other. Then, keeping the heel of your rear foot solidly on the ground, bend your front knee and press your hips forward until you feel a tug in the calf of your rear leg. You can support yourself by leaning against a wall or some other sturdy object. Hold the stretch for about twenty seconds, then gently stretch a little bit more. Then switch legs.

If you keep your back knee straight, you stretch not only your Achilles tendon in that leg, but the largest part of your calf muscle, the gastrocnemius, as well. If you bend your knee, you stretch the tendon and the smaller portion of the calf muscle, the soleus. To be thorough about it, you should do the stretch once with the knee straight and once with the knee bent.

Quadriceps Stretch

The quadriceps, the large muscle in the front of the thigh, is the biggest and strongest muscle in the body. It allows you to straighten your leg. Place your hand on the top of your thigh, and you'll feel your quadriceps tense and contract every time you take a step.

To stretch the quadriceps, stand up and bend your leg back behind your back, grab the top of your foot with your hand, and gently pull the leg up toward your buttocks. Make sure that you grab your foot with the *opposite* hand—right foot, left hand; left foot, right hand. That's very important, since otherwise you can injure your knee while bending it. You don't need to bend your leg to the point that your foot actually touches your buttocks. Simply pull until you feel the tug. Then hold for about twenty seconds, gently pull a little more, and go to the next leg.

Quadriceps stretch

Hamstring Stretch

The hamstring is the large muscle in the back of the thigh. It complements the quadriceps by allowing you to bend your leg. So when the quads contract, the hamstrings stretch and vice versa. If you place your hand on the back of your thigh as you walk, you can feel the hamstrings stretching and contracting with each step.

To stretch the hamstrings, extend your leg in front of you and rest it on a chair or low table. Then slowly bend your body over the leg until you feel the tug in your hamstrings. Hold for about twenty seconds, then bend a little more. Then switch to the other leg.

Hamstring stretch

Groin Stretch

The fanlike muscles in your groin and upper thigh are called adductors, and they're responsible for pulling your legs together.

They also work to keep your hip stable while you're PaceWalking or doing a host of other activities. And while the adductors may not be as vitally involved as some other muscles in the process of PaceWalking, it can be a good idea to stretch them before exercising, since adductor injuries can be awful to deal with. Some people hurt for years without getting better. It's an injury to be avoided, and stretching is one way to help do that.

A groin stretch is much like a hamstring stretch. Extend your leg and rest it on a chair or low table. But instead of bending over the leg, turn your body away from it. You should feel a tug in the groin. Hold the stretch for twenty seconds or so, then stretch a little more. Then go on to the other leg. And, as always, keep the stretches slow and gentle.

Groin stretch

Back and Spine Twist

It goes without saying that your back is vitally important in whatever you do. Back problems, especially in the lower back, and particularly in men, are some of the most visible and bothersome of all injuries, whether exercise related or not. It doesn't pay to neglect or misuse your back.

All of this makes me happy to say that PaceWalking puts little strain on your back. Any exercise done against gravity—running, aerobic dancing, tennis, and so on—will put at least *some* strain on your back, but PaceWalking is kinder to your poor, overworked back than any of these. Because of the gentle nature of PaceWalking, the strain on the lower back is minimized. (Nothing, of course, is easier on the body than activities in which gravity is neutralized,

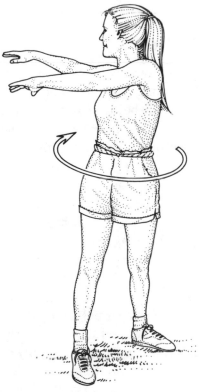

Side-to-side back stretch

such as swimming or other water-buoyed exercise like water aerobics. These activities cause less impact and jarring. But that very lack of impact can be a problem, as bones tend to lose density and strength when they're not called upon to support the body against gravity.)

All that's needed before or after PaceWalking, then, are a few slow stretches. You can stretch your back and spine from side to side by firmly planting your feet at about shoulder width, pointed ahead and parallel to one another, and then slowly and gently twisting your torso and head as though taking a look at what's behind you. Keep your arms in front of you as you turn. You should feel that stretch in your entire torso, from the lower back to your chest. Hold the stretch for about twenty seconds, then slowly twist around to the other side. Repeat the stretch again, one side to the other.

Back and Spine Stretch

This one can feel awfully good, especially after your workout when you may be feeling a bit sore and stiff. And it's one of the safest stretches possible because you let gravity do the work for you. Stand with your feet approximately shoulder width apart and slowly bend forward from the hips. Continue to let gravity pull you down—*don't* force it—until you feel the stretch in your lower back (you'll feel it in your hips and hamstrings, too). Hang there for about twenty seconds, then gently bend down a bit more. It feels good and is very good for your lower back.

Let your arms relax and hang down, and breathe slowly and deeply. And keep your legs bent, just a little. It doesn't matter how far down you can go, as long as you feel the stretch. Whether you're able to touch your toes or the floor doesn't matter in the least.

When done, *don't* try to straighten up the way you came down. Let your legs straighten you, rather than the smaller and more easily injured muscles in the lower back. Simply bend your knees and tilt back until your torso is pretty much upright. Then straighten your knees. That's the easy way to get back up, *and* the safe way.

Hanging back stretch

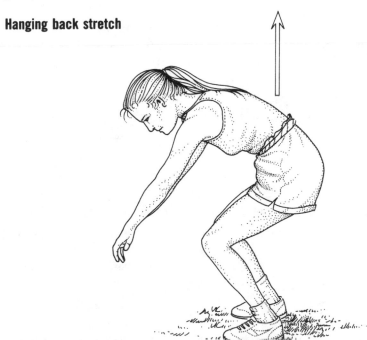

Bending your knees to straighten up from a back stretch

Curl-ups

Curl-ups are *not* stretches, but they're worth including here because of all the good they can do for your back.

My *back*, you say? How can stomach exercises be good for my back?

Well, it's easy to forget (unless you're injured, that is) that everything in the body is connected. The stomach and back muscles have in common the backbone and rib cage; muscles that pull on one end of this arrangement affect the muscles at the other end. Your stomach and back muscles complement each other, and your body depends on a proper balance between them. But if one set of muscles grows disproportionally strong, or weak, it can throw this crucial balance out of whack. The result is pain and discomfort.

That often means back problems. Because back muscles are larger and more powerful than stomach muscles, and because most people's stomach muscles are comparatively weak anyhow, these disproportionally strong back muscles can bend your back out of shape—literally. The antidote to that state of affairs is to strengthen your stomach muscles. The best, and easiest, way to do that is by doing curl-ups.

Whenever you feel your back beginning to ache or tighten up, or as a precaution against it doing so, you can do a few curl-ups. Here's how:

Lie on your back on the floor with your hands resting together over the lower part of your chest, knees bent, and feet flat on the floor. Tilt your pelvis, thereby pressing the small of your back into the floor. Then slowly curl your head and shoulders up far enough that your shoulder blades just clear the floor. Hold it for a moment, the slowly curl back down. If you're doing it right, you should feel the tug in your stomach and nowhere else.

It's not important how many curl-ups you can do (they're harder than they look; don't be disappointed if you can only do a few), only that you do them right. And "right" means with the small of your back flush against the floor. The minute you feel your back

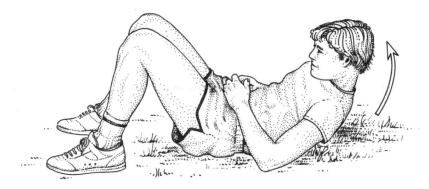

Curl-ups

begin to arch, stop; your muscles are getting tired. And when you start doing the curl-ups quickly so as to do more of them, stop. Curl-ups must be done slowly, with a flat back. That way you'll strengthen your stomach muscles and provide better support for your aching back. Other exercises, like conventional sit-ups, will strengthen various parts of your body, but none will so effectively strengthen your stomach muscles alone, and therefore do so much good for your back.

Shoulder and Arm Stretches

As we'll see in a few minutes, one of the things that distinguishes PaceWalking from plain old walking is the arm swing. In PaceWalking, a vigorous, exaggerated arm swing helps push your heart rate into the aerobic range. So, it may be a good idea to stretch your arms and shoulders.

Arm Rotations

Rotating your arms can loosen up the shoulder joint. Make the rotations big ones, as though your arm were a windmill. Go clock-

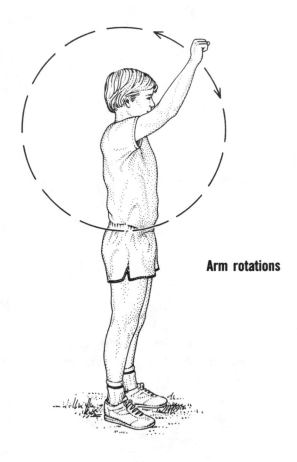

Arm rotations

wise and counterclockwise, as much as feels good and at a speed that is comfortable. The important thing is *not to do anything that hurts*. If you've had shoulder problems, be gentle with yourself. If the rotations hurt at all, don't bother doing them.

Arm Sawing

This is one of the best exercises you can do to stretch as well as strengthen your shoulder. And for PaceWalkers it's particularly good because it approximates the arm swings you'll be doing during your workout.

Stand up straight and begin sawing. Pretend you're at one end of a double-handled saw, and work through that log. Back and

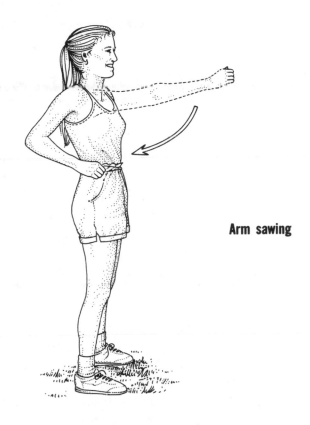

Arm sawing

forth, back and forth. Again, do as many repetitions as feel good, but don't do anything that hurts. The more repetitions you can do, the more your range of motion will increase—preparing you for PaceWalking-style arm swings. The exercise stretches and strengthens at the same time, and it puts your elbow through a complete range of motion as well.

Once you're done on one side, go on to the other side. And if you like, do both sides at once. Pretend that you have a saw in each hand and go to work. Extend one arm while the other is back, then vice versa. Doing the exercise two-handed also provides more movement to the back, further approximating what you'll actually be doing while PaceWalking.

CHAPTER 4

The PaceWalking Program

I've based the philosophy of the PaceWalking Program—or PWP, for short—on the approach to aerobic sports training developed by the great middle-distance running coach from the University of Oregon, Bill Bowerman. I've modified his famous Ten Principles slightly to apply directly to PaceWalking. Here they are:

1. Training must be regular, based on a long-term plan.
2. The work load must be balanced.
3. Overtraining, which can lead to fatigue, injury, and loss of desire, must be avoided.
4. Training schedules should be set up with a hard/easy rotation, both from day to day and more generally over time.
5. Moderation, in attitude and deed, is the key.
6. Rest should be regularly scheduled.
7. A balanced diet is essential.
8. Body mechanics should be such that the exercise is as efficient as possible.
9. You must know your goals, and they must be realistic ones.
10. Working out should be fun, whenever possible.

As you can see, these principles are based on an appreciation of and a respect for the body. They aim toward long-term, lasting satisfaction rather than immediate, more spectacular results. And they recognize that exercise is a personal thing.

All of these principles are important. The PaceWalking schedules that follow incorporate principles 1 to 6, so if you follow them reasonably faithfully you'll satisfy those requirements without even having to worry about them. I discuss principle 7 in chapter 10, and principle 8 has already shown up in the section on the PaceWalking gait, in chapter 3. But perhaps the most important of all are principles 9 and 10, which I've already talked about in chapters 2 and 3, respectively. It's with these that *you*—you as a unique person—come in. If you don't know *why* you're exercising, and if the reason is not a realistic one, you may never be satisfied with the results.

Of course, you might change your goals as you go along; that often happens as a person becomes more accustomed to working out and more knowledgeable about its possibilities. (This certainly happened to me as I traveled the road from three-times-a-week runner to Ironman-distance triathlete.) Also, your goals might be somewhat vague, in the beginning or later on. "I'm PaceWalking because I want to feel good," is a perfectly valid goal, and one that more likely than not is realistic and realizable. It's just that you should have some goal in mind to help you make the most of your efforts.

That's not to say that a good goal, perhaps even the best of all, might not be, "I'm PaceWalking because I enjoy it." *Working out should be fun, whenever possible.* Otherwise, why bother? Pain is *not* gain—not pain of the mind and spirit, that is. *Joy* is gain. And you'll gain most from your exercising if the strongest motivation of all is the enjoyment you feel in it. Happily for those of us who exercise, one of the most enjoyable activities of all is taking a good, brisk walk—especially so in a pleasant environment. I've found that PaceWalking satisfies this last and most important principle wonderfully well. It's simply a lot of fun.

PaceWalking Program Principles

The "Three-Hour Max" for Aerobic Fitness

My training program works up to an average of three hours of PaceWalking per week, but it doesn't go beyond that total. There are other programs that do, of course. Why do I stop at three? Because three hours of good exercise a week is all anyone needs to receive the maximum health benefit from aerobic exercise.

The American College of Sports Medicine has established that the minimum amount of exercise needed to provide aerobic health benefits is a twenty-minute period for three to four times a week. That adds up to an hour and twenty minutes a week for steady, lasting aerobic benefits. But that's not to say you can't exercise more than that and realize correspondingly increased health benefits—up to a point. That maximum point is at about twice as much exercise, or two and a half to three hours a week. Such is the result of research done by Dr. Kenneth Cooper. Beyond three hours a week, the health benefits don't keep pace with the time put in. They may still increase as you exercise more, but they won't increase by much, and then you begin to put yourself at risk of overuse injury.

Fitness is a different matter. And here's where it's important to make a distinction between health and fitness. Health is a state of well-being and optimum functioning characterized by the absence of disease and a relatively low risk of developing disease in the future. For example, one of these risks is high blood pressure; exercise can do a great deal to help reduce that risk. Exercise also reduces the risk of heart disease, sudden death during exertion, diabetes, osteoporosis, obesity, and, possibly, cancer; and it's useful in managing existing cases of a number of these problems as well as others, including cigarette smoking, substance abuse, and poorly managed stress.

Fitness, on the other hand, is the ability to do physical work over a period of time: for example, swim a certain number of laps, run so many miles, or PaceWalk so far and for so long a time. Fitness involves healthy cardiovascular and musculoskeletal systems that are *trained* to work together to accomplish the task at hand. Fitness means *applying* health toward a particularly active end.

Up to a certain point, well beyond three hours a week, there's a fairly direct connection between the amount of aerobic exercise that you do and your level of fitness. So for reasons of *fitness,* the three-hour-a-week standard does not apply. If you want to, you can keep exercising and keep increasing your fitness level. But you eventually reach a fitness limit, too. For example, exercise physiologist Dr. David Costill of Ball State University has found that improvements in fitness accompany increases in running mileage up into the eight- to ten-hour-per-week range, but tail off quickly after that. But now we're talking about a level of fitness suitable for fast marathon running. Three hours a week is plenty for a level of fitness that will completely satisfy most people; and two hours a week will stand you in very good stead. You don't need to do more than that unless your goal is more than a good general level of health and fitness. Just another reason why it's so important to know *why* you're exercising.

So I recommend three hours per week, tops. The schedules reflect that approach. You can use them in any way that suits you. Just be sure you know your reasons and goals, one way or another.

Medical Evaluation

If you're a nonexerciser who's starting the PaceWalking program from scratch, I would recommend having a medical evaluation first. I know a complete evaluation is neither cheap nor quick, and if you're just starting out and aren't sure if you want to stick with the program, you may be even less anxious to spend the money and time. So use your own best judgment here. But if you have any of the following twelve problems, you definitely should get an exam before starting an exercise program.

1. High blood pressure
2. High blood cholesterol
3. Cigarette smoking
4. Pain or pressure in your chest when you exert yourself
5. History of heart disease in parents or siblings
6. More than 20 percent over normal weight

7. Completely sedentary life-style in recent years
8. Any history of lung problems
9. Prescribed medication used on a regular basis
10. Abuse of drugs or alcohol
11. Any bone or joint problem
12. Any other chronic illness, such as diabetes

Any of these problems could lead to greater, even life-threatening problems. See a doctor to be assured that it's safe for you to exercise in the first place and to develop a gradual program ultimately leading to more exercise.

It just so happens that one of the frequently prescribed treatments for many of these problems is exercise—more specifically, walking. For example, how many doctors have encouraged high-blood-pressure sufferers to take a good, brisk walk as a way to help bring their blood pressure down? And how many overweight people have been urged to exercise their pounds away? For a number of them, the way to start is by taking a good walk. PaceWalking is just the thing to combat many of these ills. But if you have one, it is best to start out under medical supervision.

You may run into doctors who warn you that intelligent exercise is either not good for you, generally bad for you, or—in extreme cases—might harm you a great deal. (Most physicians, though, no matter how uncomfortable they may be with other kinds of exercise, will give you little argument about the virtues of PaceWalking—at least if you don't say the "Pace" part too loudly.)

If you're not satisfied with the level of knowledge your doctor exhibits in relation to aerobic activity, politely but firmly ask for a referral to someone with the proper experience and skills to help you out. You may want to go directly to a cardiofitness center for an evaluation. These centers are appearing in increasing numbers all around the country, in private physicians' offices and in hospitals. They are usually well-staffed and able to help you. They will also be happy to keep your personal physician informed of their findings and recommendations.

The Schedules

What follows are four different PaceWalking training programs: Introductory, Developmental, Maintenance, and Maintenance Plus. Each schedule is thirteen weeks long. Each consists of three to four workouts per week, along with the recommended number of PaceWalking minutes for each workout. And there's also a blank program form, the Design-Your-Own Program. After you've become a regular PaceWalker, you might want to design a personalized schedule. (You also might want to make photocopies of the blank form before writing on it.)

Do not feel bound to follow these programs to the letter. They're guides, not requirements. They do provide a well-thought-out plan for those of you who want to follow them down to the minute. There's no harm in that, certainly, but if you do no more than stay within their general parameters, they'll still work for you. However, that means not skipping the midweek workouts and cramming everything into weekends. It means that if you miss a session—which is no sin—you don't make it up all at once during the next session. An occasional miss will not harm you; if you do want to make it up, spread the makeup minutes over several workout sessions.

It won't hurt to do two workouts in a row during the week. For example, if you miss a Tuesday because of bad weather or travel or work demands, you can do that workout on Wednesday and still do your Thursday workout as well. You can also change the time of day during which you do your workouts, without harm. If you usually exercise in the morning, but on a particular day it works better for you to exercise later on, do it that way. I am a morning regular, but when traveling on business I often do my workouts in the evening. The point is that, one way or another, I get most of them in.

The four progams are designed to connect with each other in a logical sequence. The Introductory Program is for beginners. The Developmental Program gets you up to the three-hour maximum level. The Maintenance Program pretty much keeps you at that health and fitness level through a schedule of two hours per week.

And the Maintenance Plus Program puts you at the upper level in a steady, ongoing way. If you feel like doing more than three hours of PaceWalking per week, design your own schedule (and consider going to five workouts per week in order to keep individual sessions at a reasonable length).

If you're already a walker, or if you're coming to PaceWalking from another aerobic sport, don't think that you have to begin with the Introductory Program. Just walk in at the point in any of the programs that most closely matches the length and frequency of your previous workouts. And go on from there.

The Introductory Program— Starting from Scratch

If you've never done any aerobic exercise, or haven't done any for quite a while, this is where to start. The Introductory Program is designed to ease you into PaceWalking.

Ease is the critical word here. If you're anything like me, you tend to jump into things with both feet, especially those things that you're enthusiastic about, rather than *easing* into them gradually. With some things, such an all-or-nothing approach may work just fine. But exercise is not one of those things. The body just doesn't take kindly to being thrown into activities for which it's not pre-pared. And the older we become, the more the body protests the introduction of new and demanding behavior. At the least, you'll hurt afterwards and actually tear down your body a bit rather than build it up right away. And if your body protests too much, the result can be an injury. It's very important to move *gradually* into any new exercise activities.

PaceWalking is good for the heart and easy on the body. But even so, you'll probably hurt a little during and afterwards. Most likely, you'll experience two different varieties of pain. If you're just starting out, you'll encounter some natural stiffness and "morning after" pain, as muscles you may not have used since childhood are

Introductory Program
(Times in Minutes)

Week	M	T	W	Th	F	S	S	Total	
1	Off	10	Off	10	Off	Off	10	30	Ordinary
2	Off	10	Off	10	Off	Off	10	30	Walking
3	Off	20	Off	20	Off	Off	20	60	Ordinary
4	Off	20	Off	20	Off	Off	20	60	Walking
5	Off	20	Off	20	Off	Off	20	60	Fast
6	Off	20	Off	20	Off	Off	20	60	Walking
7	Off	20	Off	20	Off	Off	30	70	Fast
8	Off	20	Off	20	Off	Off	30	70	Walking
9	Off	20	Off	20	Off	Off	20	60	PaceWalking
10	Off	20	Off	20	Off	Off	30	70	
11	Off	20	Off	30	Off	Off	30	80	PaceWalking
12	Off	20	Off	30	Off	Off	30	80	
13	Off	30	Off	30	Off	Off	30	90	PaceWalking

called into action. That's normal—don't be alarmed. If you follow the program, which eases you into PaceWalking very gently, you shouldn't have too much discomfort. And here's where stretching *afterwards* can make a big difference. Muscles that are tired tend to contract; that makes them hurt all the more. Stretching will help your muscles stay relaxed and loose—in turn, helping you stay pain free.

Once you're well into your PaceWalking in the later weeks of the Introductory Program, and you're getting your speed up and incorporating a vigorous arm swing, you may well experience some pain in your legs, upper arms, and shoulders. (These mild pains have little in common with the twisting, pounding, and jarring in the legs that accompanies running, or the burn in the thighs that bikers experience grinding up a steep hill.) That, too, is to be expected. Even PaceWalking, as gentle as it is, will make your body hurt at least a little. "No pain, no gain" is the general idea, but it doesn't quite say it. A better motto for PaceWalking would be, "Not much pain brings a great deal of gain." And here, again, stretching afterwards may help keep the hurt to a minimum.

The Introductory Program shows you how to begin gradually. As you can see, for the first two weeks you'll just take a ten-minute walk, three times a week. What could be *easier*? You don't have to worry about speed or heart rate—not yet. Just walk at a comfortable pace for ten minutes—or a bit more, if you feel like it. This set is designed to help you limber up and become accustomed to a regular pattern of workouts.

This last thought is the key: a regular pattern of workouts. For many people who are trying to become exercisers, getting onto a regular schedule is the single hardest thing to do. It may be easy enough to hit it a lick every once in a while, but *regularly*? Even when you may not feel like it? And when the weather might not be perfect? And when there are so many other things to do? Or, in many cases, not do?

But once you do work into a regular schedule, a strange thing will begin to happen: You'll start regretting the occasional missed workout. The rhythm of it all becomes part of you; break the rhythm and something important goes out of your day. You may start looking forward to your workouts with an interest, even an eagerness you never thought possible.

For the next two weeks, you'll walk twice as much—twenty minutes at a time—and still at a comfortable pace. No reason to push yourself at this point. Just become accustomed to working out regularly. And this is a good time to scout out enjoyable routes and settings. It's a time to prepare both mind and body for the more concentrated workouts to come.

In weeks five and six, you'll move to a different level. You don't increase the time spent working out, but you do increase the speed of your walking. But fast walking does not mean PaceWalking. Just continue walking as before, picking up the pace a little. You don't have to worry about arm swing, you don't have to take your pulse—not yet. Just walk a little faster, all the time aiming at smoothness and relaxation.

During weeks seven and eight, you'll continue your fast walking, but you'll add another ten minutes to your total workout time. By now you're getting in shape to begin PaceWalking.

By week nine, you're ready to PaceWalk. You might go back and read over the sections on gait and arm swing. Now is when *how* you walk becomes important, because you want to drive your heart rate into the aerobic range. You might want to brush up by taking a quick look back over the sections in chapter 3, "How to Determine Your Aerobic Heart Rate" (page 26) and "How to Measure Your Heart Rate" (page 28). That done, you're ready to go.

Don't worry about speed. Just work at getting the gait and the arm swing under control—especially the arm swing. At first it can feel somewhat awkward to swing your arms with such gusto; now's the time to get used to it. Week nine drops the amount of time spent exercising by ten minutes, but don't worry; just the fact that you're beginning to actually PaceWalk will more than make up for the decrease. The arm swing is deceivingly vigorous. If you doubt that, just stand in place and swing your arms forcefully—you'll know you're exercising. Combine that kind of activity with actually walking, and the result is PaceWalking, which gives you a good, solid aerobic workout.

Take your pulse about halfway through your PaceWalk and then once again at the end. You'll probably find that it's comfortably in the aerobic range. If not, speed up your pace and accentuate your arm swing. In fact, a more vigorous arm swing alone may do the job for you. But don't drive your heart rate too high. Remember, once you're above 85 percent of your maximum, it's more than you need. Slow down a bit or swing your arms a little less energetically until you find the combination that works for you. For most PaceWalkers a heart rate that is 70 to 75 percent of 220 minus your age is ideal. It may take some experimenting, but sooner or later you'll get it. Then continue at that pace for the rest of your workout, and for the rest of the workouts during the week.

An important caution: *If your heart rate consistently runs higher than 85 percent of maximum, or you feel palpitations in your chest or pain in your chest, arms, or jaw, stop your workout. And don't begin again until you see a doctor.* These can be signs of heart disease. They're nothing to fool around with or ignore.

Weeks ten through thirteen of the Introductory Program offer increasingly long PaceWalking workouts. By the time you're done with week thirteen, you'll be PaceWalking for an hour and a half a week and will begin to feel like a pro. You should have a sense of what pace works well for you and how vigorously you need to swing your arms in order to achieve an aerobic heart rate. You'll be an old hand at taking your pulse, and will most likely have found a PaceWalking route or two that help make your workout a pleasure. And, if all has gone well, you've probably discovered a few other things.

First, you'll have a good idea whether this PaceWalking business agrees with you or not. It doesn't for everyone, you know; and if you're one of those people—well—better to find out sooner than later. Thirteen weeks, five of them actually PaceWalking, is enough to give you a taste for the activity. If it's not for you, don't feel bad. There are lots of other kinds of aerobic exercise.

If PaceWalking is your cup of tea, however, by now you will probably have developed the beginnings of a steady, disciplined approach to aerobic exercise—by far the best way to go about it. You will have been exercising for thirteen weeks, and even if you haven't followed the Introductory Program to the letter, you've been doing fairly regular workouts over an extended period of time. You will have begun to train your body in this repetitive, regular mode. You'll probably find that you look forward to each session, feel better afterwards—and feel as though you've missed something if you don't get to your workout on any particular day. In other words, you may experience the first inklings of that peculiar condition shared by so many of us who exercise: You get hooked.

And, best of all, you may experience the beginnings of why you probably started exercising in the first place: results. I venture to say that already you will notice the difference in your stamina. You probably will get out of breath less easily, feel like sitting this one out less readily. It may be that you will feel more energetic in general. And maybe—just maybe—you will have already lost a pound or two or a fraction of an inch around your waist. If not, be patient; such results will come. You're laying a foundation that will always be there for you, no matter what kind of exercise you do. And as far as PaceWalking is concerned, you're on your way. Ready for the next step.

Again, all these programs are purposely designed to set you on your way slowly and easily. If you find the progress too slow, don't feel you have to follow the schedule minute by minute, day by day, week by week. Use it as a guide. You may want to add minutes, add workouts, even get to actual PaceWalking more quickly. If so, that's fine. But, be careful not to overdo it. If in doubt, move too slowly rather than too quickly. You can always speed up later on.

The Developmental Program

The second part of the PWP, the Developmental Program, is the transition stage—the thirteen weeks that take you from experienced beginner to young veteran, ready to maintain your PaceWalking for as long as it suits you. By the time you're done with this stage, you'll have twenty-six solid weeks under your belt, and the habits and skills you began to solidify in the Introductory Program will have become an integral part of your makeup. You'll have developed to the point that you're PaceWalking two to three hours a week regularly and are able to sustain that pace indefinitely.

But, before getting started with all that, the Developmental Program begins with a week off. If you look ahead, you'll see that all subsequent programs begin with a week off. Because one of the biggest problems for anyone who exercises regularly is burn-out. You get to the point where you're reasonably comfortable with what you're doing. You may be seeing and feeling real results, but the initial

Developmental Program
(PaceWalking)
(Times in Minutes)

Week	M	T	W	Th	F	S	S	Total
1	Off	Off	Off	Off	Off	Off	Off	Off
2	Off	20	Off	20	Off	Off	20	60
3	Off	20	Off	20	Off	20	20	80
4	Off	20	Off	20	Off	20	30	90
5	Off	20	Off	30	Off	20	30	100
6	Off	20	Off	30	Off	20	40	110
7	Off	30	Off	30	Off	30	30	120
8	Off	30	Off	30	Off	30	40	130
9	Off	30	Off	40	Off	30	40	140
10	Off	30	Off	40	Off	30	50	150
11	Off	40	Off	30	Off	30	60	160
12	Off	40	Off	30	Off	40	60	170
13	Off	30	Off	40	Off	50	60	180

challenge and novelty have worn off a bit. The routine rears its boring head, and you think, "What am I doing, anyhow?" Burn-out. And the best way to deal with burn-out is to take some time off *before* it happens. That's one reason each program begins with time off.

The other reason is that not only do the mind and spirit require rest and variety, but so does the body. You've been working your muscles and bones and cardiovascular system for thirteen weeks, with an intensity and regularity that most likely you've never experienced before. Your body, too, could use some time off.

So use the week off to forget all about PaceWalking. Do other things, or do nothing at all. Then, when the next week rolls around and you're again ready to go, the likelihood is that you'll come back with renewed vigor and enthusiasm. But don't try to start up at the same level at which you left off—that's important. Notice that weeks two and three of the Developmental Program require less exercise time than the last week of the Introductory Program. The reasoning behind this reduced demand is that while taking time off is good for you, body and spirit, it slows down a bit your ability to PaceWalk. You simply can't take time off and expect to resume at the same rate. To do so would put extra strain on muscles, bones, heart, and blood vessels that have just had the luxury of a week's vacation. It takes time to get back—but less time than it took to get there in the first place.

Weeks two and three are *getting back* weeks—a time to ease your body back to the level of condition it enjoyed a couple of weeks ago. Once you hit week four, you'll be back to where you left off. And weeks five and onward steadily build from there. By the time you're doing week thirteen's schedule, you'll be PaceWalking three hours per week.

Notice also that workouts within the weeks themselves vary in length. For example, workouts for week ten run from thirty minutes to forty to thirty to fifty. And nowhere in the PaceWalking Program do I suggest lengthy workouts back to back. Just as it's a good idea to take time off between workouts, whether it be an entire week or a day off, it's a good idea to alternate relatively short and long workouts, easy and hard workouts. The change gives the body—and mind—a chance to recover and build to the next. (Again, I'm indebted to Bill Bowerman.)

From the third week on, you'll be doing four workouts a week. That's a step up from the Introductory Program's three workouts. This regimen will prepare you for both the Maintenance Program, which requires four workouts every other week, and the Maintenance Plus, which requires four workouts every week. And because PWP should be as doable and convenient as possible, during most weeks I've scheduled more than half the total minutes on the weekend days. But if you're one of those people who has time during the week as well, you can easily rearrange the schedule to meet your own needs. Just use the Design-Your-Own Program and fill in the blanks as you see fit.

The Developmental Program maxes out at three hours. Anyone can safely and comfortably reach that level. But you don't have to. If you already know that you're eventually going to use the two-hours-per-week Maintenance Program on a regular basis, rather than the Maintenance Plus Program, there's no need to work out three hours per week. The Maintenance Program averages two hours per week (the aerobic equivalent of running twelve to fifteen miles per week, for those of you who want to compare what you're doing with that of your running friends). That's certainly enough to keep anyone healthy and fit—and to prepare for it you don't need to work out more than that amount of time. If the Maintenance Program is your goal, when you finish week nine of the Developmental Program, don't go on to the next level. Simply drop back to week six and continue through to week nine once again, substituting that workout sequence for the recommended weeks ten through thirteen.

Whichever path you take, you'll be using the last few weeks to get your technique down and your speed up. And by the time you finish all thirteen weeks, you'll most likely discover that you're in better shape than you ever have been. You'll also find that to keep your heart rate in the aerobic range, you have to work harder than ever before. That's the irony of getting in shape: The more fit you are, the more efficiently your body functions, and the harder it is to boost your heart rate up to where you want it. (By now it should be abundantly clear how important that arm swing really is.)

When you finish the Developmental Program, give yourself a hearty pat on the back. You are now a PaceWalker. You've been through twenty-six solid weeks of training; you've learned a new sport. You're on your way to becoming aerobically healthy and fit. And the gains that were little more than hints at the end of the Introductory Program are now becoming readily apparent. If you haven't yet lost weight, you've probably redistributed some of it and firmed up some more. You don't get out of breath nearly as easily as you used to. Your stamina has increased noticeably, not only during PaceWalking but in any activity. That's one of the pleasures of aerobic exercise—the benefits spill over into the rest of our lives. I daresay your tennis game is better, or your swimming, or your ability to work in the garden or climb the stairs. If you're not looking better and feeling better about yourself, something's definitely wrong.

So, reward yourself—you've really accomplished something! Go out and buy that nifty sports outfit you've been eyeing all this time. Go away for a weekend, with or without PaceWalking. Indulge in that pie à la mode or hot fudge sundae you've been dutifully putting off for the last few months.

The Maintenance and Maintenance Plus Programs, and the Design-Your-Own Program

From now on, the goals you set for your aerobic conditioning become more important than ever. You've gotten to the point at which you can tailor your exercise schedule to suit your own needs and desires. You've done the basic, working up, getting in shape stuff—the hardest work, really. Now you *are* in shape. And the question becomes, what kind of shape do you want to remain in?

If you like your general degree of health and fitness and want to stay there, and if you like the pace and length of your PaceWalks as they are, then the Maintenance Program may be for you. The program is designed to *maintain* your general fitness level, to continue the length and frequency of your workouts (with some variety, of course), and keep you toned and healthy. But if you're ready for more—for a somewhat more rigorous program and for an added degree of fitness—then the Maintenance Plus Program might be the way to go. The latter builds on what you've accomplished so far by increasing both the frequency and total time spent in PaceWalking.

And if neither of these programs appeals to you, or if you try either or both and find that they don't quite meet your particular needs, then the Design-Your-Own Program is ready and waiting. After all, by now you're the expert. No one knows your own body as you do. It may be time for you to be your own coach and student.

The Maintenance Program

Week one is a week off. Take a rest. Relax. Savor what you've accomplished.

Maintenance
PaceWalking
(Times in Minutes)

Week	M	T	W	Th	F	S	S	Total
1	Off	Off	Off	Off	Off	Off	Off	Off
2	Off	30	Off	30	Off	40	Off	100
3	30	Off	40	Off	20	Off	40	130
4	Off	40	Off	30	Off	40	Off	110
5	30	Off	40	Off	20	Off	40	130
6	Off	40	Off	30	Off	60	Off	130
7	20	Off	30	Off	30	Off	40	120
8	Off	40	Off	30	Off	50	Off	120
9	20	Off	40	Off	20	Off	60	140
10	Off	30	Off	30	Off	40	Off	100
11	20	Off	30	Off	20	Off	40	110
12	Off	40	Off	30	Off	60	Off	130
13	20	Off	30	Off	30	Off	40	120

Average: 120 minutes per week for twelve weeks

Week two gets you back to work, but a reduced amount of work. At the end of the Developmental Program you were doing either two hours and twenty minutes or three hours of PaceWalking a week, depending on your preference. Now you'll start again with just an hour and forty minutes a week. And then, you'll average two hours a week. This is about the amount of time that most regular runners in the country put in per week. It is almost double the American College of Sports Medicine's minimum recommended time for lasting aerobic health and fitness. It'll keep you in the kind of condition you've achieved up to now.

As you can see, the Maintenance Program follows an every-other-day schedule—three days of PaceWalking one week, four days the next. This on-again, off-again approach is based on the fact that muscles that have worked hard generally take about forty-eight hours to recover. This kind of every-other-day schedule has been standard among weight lifters for years. It's also good for the mind and spirit; variety helps keep us from burning out.

This balanced, moderate program may be just the approach that works for you. Try it and see. If it isn't quite right, you may want to design your own. Or you may want to try something a little more demanding: Maintenance Plus.

Maintenance Plus Program

It's crunch time. Here's where you get a chance to strut your stuff, to really step out and PaceWalk. The Maintenance Plus Program averages three hours of exercise a week, with a high of three and a half hours and a low of two and a half. There are four workouts a week in the program, with more than half the total minutes of each week concentrated in the two weekend days. And, of course, the whole business begins with a week off and a relatively reduced first week of PaceWalking.

Maintenance Plus
PaceWalking
(Times in Minutes)

Week	M	T	W	Th	F	S	S	Total
1	Off	Off	Off	Off	Off	Off	Off	Off
2	Off	30	Off	40	Off	30	50	150
3	Off	30	Off	50	Off	40	60	180
4	Off	40	Off	40	Off	50	80	210
5	Off	30	Off	50	Off	40	60	180
6	Off	50	Off	30	Off	50	70	200
7	Off	40	Off	30	Off	30	60	160
8	Off	30	Off	50	Off	40	60	180
9	Off	30	Off	40	Off	30	50	150
10	Off	30	Off	50	Off	40	50	170
11	Off	40	Off	30	Off	50	70	190
12	Off	40	Off	40	Off	50	80	210
13	Off	30	Off	50	Off	40	60	180

Average: 180 minutes per week for twelve weeks

Some PaceWalkers find this program to be just about their speed. Some prefer to alternate thirteen-week blocks between Maintenance and Maintenance Plus. Whichever group you fall into, you can be certain that continuing to PaceWalk will bring lasting enjoyment and health benefits. But I have a feeling that by now you don't need to be told that. PaceWalkers tend to become hooked and need no convincing. And they often become enthusiastic advertisements for the value of aerobic exercise, no matter what kind. I should know—it happened to me.

Design-Your-Own Program

All right, go to it! Be imaginative, creative, easy, or tough on yourself. But remember, on and off, easy and hard, variety as well as consistency—that's the name of the PaceWalking game.

Design-Your-Own PaceWalking Program (Times in Minutes)

Week	M	T	W	Th	F	S	S	Total
1	Off	Off	Off	Off	Off	Off	Off	Off
2								
3								
4								
5								
6								
7								
8								
9								
10								
11								
12								
13								

Making a Commitment to PaceWalking

Chapters 3 and 4 contain everything you need to get started and stay started. They advise you as to what equipment you need to PaceWalk (very little), where to PaceWalk, when to PaceWalk, how to PaceWalk. They suggest the benefits of PaceWalking and the joys. They alert you as to the possible problems and how to deal with them. And they provide detailed programs to enable you to begin with confidence and eventually to chart your own PaceWalking path. What they don't do—and can't do—is provide you with the motivation to get going and stay with it. No book can do that. The only one who can do that is you.

You are the one who has to get up a bit earlier in the morning, or shorten your lunch hour, or postpone dinner until you're finished with your workout. You're the one who has to put up with the inevitable aches and pains, cold or hot or wet or icy days, the overwhelming feeling of just not wanting to go out and do it. You're the one who has to make the commitment to exercise.

It's necessary to make a commitment. Exercise can be a lot of fun, yes; and the benefits are real and lasting, true. Exercise can be addicting—countless people have testified to that. I'm a prime example. Just a few years ago I did no exercise and had no plans to start. Now I'm so enthusiastic about it that I'm writing this, my second book on exercising. But still, in the best of situations, there are times when you just don't want to do it. There are times when it's easier to do something else, or nothing else, than go out and PaceWalk for the half hour, or hour, or hour and a half of your workout. As with just about any activity that's worthwhile, PaceWalking takes commitment. (All the more so, since aerobic exercise must be done consistently to be effective. Once in a while just won't do.)

So it's up to you. Committing yourself to the program set out here will pay handsomely. But it's you that has to make that commitment and follow through. Good luck.

CHAPTER 5

PaceWalking and Growing Older

*I*was lucky. I started exercising back in 1980. That arduous climb up the ramps at Cobo Hall in Detroit was the last straw. I knew it was time to do something about my physical condition—or, should I say, *lack* of condition. And I did it before something like a heart attack or injury *made* me face it. I started exercising because I wanted to.

I was a youngster of forty-three then; now I'm fifty-one years old. As I move into the second half-century of my life, what some people would call my "declining years," I have a foundation of health to build upon. I'm used to exercising. More than that, I don't know what I'd do without it. And I don't think of this latter part of my life as my "declining years" at all. Instead of thinking about aging, I think about growing "younger." I plan to die young, late in life. Exercising has opened my eyes to new opportunities and new challenges.

As a doctor, it's very, very interesting for me, to see the important role exercise has come to play in my life. We used to think that exercise was fine as far as it went. If you wanted to tone your muscles and increase strength, fine. If you wanted to firm up certain parts of your body and perhaps even lose a few pounds, fair enough.

But concerns of health in general were thought to be another story. That was the province of doctors and drugs, the world of malevolent little creatures like bacteria and viruses. Or it was something that was out of our control. "It's fate," we'd say when considering why one person lived a long, healthy life while another was relatively short-lived or sickly. "It lies in the lap of the gods," we'd lament as heart disease and cancer rates rose. And when it came to aging, why that was another roll of the dice. Some people aged robustly, continuing to be active and productive well into old age; others—most, really—deteriorated and declined before our eyes.

Aging was a game you couldn't win. The best you could do was fade away gracefully, find gentle activities to engage your reduced attention span, and try not to be a burden to the younger generation. And God fobid you did anything as extreme, and rash, as *exercise*. That was dangerous, prone to cause various maladies, from heart attack to injury from falling. And, if nothing else, it was just plain unseemly for oldsters to be out there acting as though they were . . . well . . . *young*.

Times have changed. And thank goodness they have. For just as exercise has transformed my life, it has also transformed the lives of a number of people, none more so than senior citizens. Not only are more and more older people finding out that it's *fun* to exercise, but research is beginning to suggest that exercise may even reverse many of the effects of aging. In other words, although there's still no fountain of youth, exercise may be the nearest thing to it. And it's been right there, available, under our noses all this time. We just seldom took advantage of it.

What Happens When We Age

Old age *is* a time of decline; moreover, the decline can actually be measured. For example, compared to a thirty-year-old, a seventy-five-year-old has approximately 80 percent as much blood flow to the brain, 70 percent as much resting heart power, 63 percent as many nerve fibers in the trunk of the body, and the ability to take in only 40 percent as much oxygen during exercise, and 36 percent the number of taste buds! There are also declines in bone mass, the quality and quantity of sleep, how acute the senses are, are how well food is digested.

After age fifty, we lose about two centimeters of height every ten years, but our ears, nose, and head actually increase in size. We generally gain weight until about fifty-five then slowly lose it thereafter. At the same time, our bones lose minerals and strength, our lungs begin to wear out, and weakened shoulder and back muscles can bring about a humpbacked appearance. Not a pretty picture. Especially when these changes come at a time in life when people often gain new appreciation for the joys and possibilities of living and finally have the time and resources to enjoy them. No wonder the song laments that "youth is wasted on the young."

Of all these changes, the most interesting to me are those that involve heart function. It's no exaggeration to say that just as PaceWalking and all other aerobic exercise first and foremost involve the heart, so do the effects of aging. As you get older, your heart has to work comparatively harder to achieve the same results as earlier in life. Each part of the cardiovascular system has to function closer to its maximum to keep up. In fact, our ability to consume oxygen—that is, how efficient we are in transporting this primary source of energy from the atmosphere through the bloodstream into every cell of our body—decreases with age about 1 percent per year, most likely from sheer loss of muscle power in the heart. The results of this reduced ability are profound, a kind of vicious circle. With less food to sustain and nurture them, muscles throughout the body shorten, thin out, and lose strength. As the muscles weaken, they no longer support our bodies as well. A body that slumps or otherwise loses structure and support often can impinge upon blood flow, further decreasing oxygen supply to the muscles. With even less oxygen available, our muscles weaken more. And so on. You just can't win.

The obvious result of all this reduction is shortness of breath and decreased coordination, flexibility, and stability—the common complaints of old age. You move more slowly, have less stamina, and take longer to recover from injuries. And you lose some of your ability to adjust to change; older people tend to want things to remain as they are. Finally, reduced blood flow contributes to one of the prime characteristics of old age—the loss of body fluids. Aging simply dries us up. From the lubricants in our joints to the fluid in the lens of our eyes (one of the reasons aging often means a need for glasses), to the loss of elasticity in bodily tissues, we lose moisture as we age.

You should be properly depressed by now. This litany of doom and gloom is enough to depress anyone. There are, however, three saving graces. The first is that these changes come upon us gradually. It's the reverse of the old story in which the child lifts the tiny calf over the fence every day. As they grow older, he continues to lift the calf until finally the child is a grown man and the calf a thousand-pound bull. And still, because growth is gradual and he never stopped lifting the animal, the man lifts the huge bull as easily as before.

The story is apocryphal, the point is not. Because these changes of aging come upon us gradually, we neither notice them or suffer from them all the time. It's only when comparing our condition to that of years ago that we're acutely aware of how much less we can do.

The second ray of light is that often these changes are not particularly significant because many parts of the body have a reserve capacity. If we're only using, say, a part of our maximum brain function anyway, the loss of 20 percent of blood flow may not be crucial—or even noticeable. A number of body systems can decline in efficiency without affecting health or performance.

Finally—and this is the really good part—a goodly number of these declines that have traditionally been considered normal by-products of aging have recently been found to be nothing of the sort. Extensive research has suggested that these "normal" examples of aging are more nearly consequences of life-style and environment. In other words, they're *not necessary*. If you change your life-style, you may be able to delay these effects for decades or *prevent them entirely*. This research suggests that many of the consequences of aging are not inevitable—not at the accelerated pace of so many of us, certainly. It suggests that we have some control over what happens to us as we age. And it implies that one of the best things we can do to exert that control and slow down or even reverse this deterioration is to *exercise*.

Disuse and Aging

One of the tip-offs that alerted research to the possibility that exercise may have a positive effect on aging came from the space program. Astronauts forced to spend a goodly amount of time in cramped, weightless quarters, with little possibility of vigorous activity and without gravity to exert its healthy tug on muscles and bones, have come home acting as though they had aged virtually overnight. They were weaker, with less muscle mass and tone. Their sense of balance was out of whack. Their bones were less dense. In some cases, they could hardly move. Their cardiovascular system had slowed down precisely as though they had entered old age.

That set researchers to thinking. Was it weightlessness that caused these changes, or was it lack of normal exercise? Was this a phenomenon of outer space, or did it mirror what happens to earthlings? What would happen to earthbound people who similarly were unable to use their bodies?

The answers were not long in coming. Studies conducted on bedridden people turned up many of the same results. It seemed as though many of the biological changes commonly attributed to aging were astonishingly similar to changes caused by extended physical inactivity. In fact, just three weeks of complete bed rest results in temporary loss of muscle tone comparable to thirty years of aging.

If it's true that if you don't use it, you lose it, then might not these so-called effects of aging *be halted and even turned around*? And if *use* is what we're after, there's nothing—*nothing*—that uses muscles and bones and all of the life systems of the body better than a program of sustained exercise.

It was exciting news. Revolutionary news. Especially for those of us who were already exercising. What it meant was that by continuing to exercise, we might be able to slow down our body's deterioration and decline. Although we might not live any longer than otherwise (although there's evidence to suggest that exercise might indeed contribute to longevity), the quality of our life might be much increased compared to what it might have been otherwise. We could stay youthful longer in the ways that matter most: health, physical capability, enjoyment of life.

Exercise and the Effects of Aging

It all comes back to the heart. As I suggested a while back, many of the unfortunate effects of aging—and of disuse, as it turns out—have to do with reduced cardiovascular capability. If your heart doesn't circulate your blood effectively, the benefits of good circulation are lessened. Chief among these is your ability to provide your body with oxygen, our primary fuel. Without our constant oxygen fix, we just don't operate very well.

But, as we've seen over and over, what's the main benefit of aerobic exercise? To increase and maintain our cardiovascular capability. By doing aerobic exercise we train our heart and cardiovascular system, build it up and keep it strong. It would seem logical that aerobic exercise might do the same for a cardiovascular system that had deteriorated through age or disuse.

Exercise not only counters the effects of disuse, it slows down the deterioration of aging as well. In fact, it was found that exercise can turn the clock back as much as twenty-five to forty-five years. And there's no time limit to all this; middle-aged to elderly, no matter when you start to exercise, you'll realize some improvement.

To wit, one study showed that a physical conditioning program improved the work capacity of seventy-year-olds by 35 percent. It also increased the amount of oxygen their cardiovascular system was able to transport to their body cells by 29 percent. Other studies discovered that exercise lowers older people's resting heart rate, increases the amount of blood their heart is able to pump with each beat, lowers their blood pressure, and reduces the tendency of their blood to form clots.

In other words, exercise can slow to a crawl the body's decreased ability to take in, circulate, and utilize oxygen—perhaps the most troublesome of the "normal" effects of aging. Exercise helps keep your heart strong and functioning efficiently. So much so, that studies have found that an exercising sixty-eight year old can have a stronger capacity to do work than a sedentary thirty-five year old.

Exercise can also reverse the characteristic bone loss of age, especially in women. A study of women in their eighties revealed that those who exercised no more than thirty minutes, three times a week, over a period of three years actually increased their bone mineral content, as compared to inactive women, who continued to lose theirs.

So the well-publicized fear of many aging women, bone loss (especially as evidenced by osteoporosis, an extreme loss of bone strength that results in a tendency to become stooped and round shouldered), can be at least partially dealt with by exercise. It's a much more certain approach than using calcium supplements and a much safer one than taking estrogen.

Exercise can increase the range of motion in the joints of older people. This is a particularly welcome finding because often one of the unhappy characteristics of aging is reduced range of motion. You used to be able to touch your toes; now you can only make it to your knees. You used to be able to rear back to smash that first serve; now you pitty-pat the ball over the net from somewhere in front of your eyes. You used to be able to turn your head to see what was happening behind you; now your whole body must swivel around. It's no fun.

Exercise helps to slow that trend. One experiment with people averaging seventy-two years of age found that just a twelve-week course of exercise was enough to increase range of motion over the entire body from as little as 8 percent to as much as 48 percent— and that's a sizable gain.

Exercise can help reduce tension and bring about real emotional satisfaction. It helps channel aggressive tendencies into useful effort. For aging people, for whom the vicissitudes of growing old can lead to frustration and unhappiness, this can be the best news.

Exercise often helps bring about other positive life-style changes for aging people. Those who are willing to exercise, and who experience the benefits of doing so, often become health conscious in other parts of their lives as well. They are more likely not to smoke or drink excessively or otherwise abuse their bodies. If the deterioration of aging (or, as seems pretty clear by now, the deterioration of *disuse*) can become a vicious circle—one problem feeding on another—the benefits of exercise can likewise produce other, more general, benefits. Do positive things in one aspect of your life, and all other areas are affected positively.

Here's a wonderful story, told to me by my neurophysiologist friend and lifelong exerciser, Irvin "Kim" Korr, that illustrates the point. When Kim was seventy-five (he's seventy-eight now and going strong), he started working on exercise programs for older people. One day he visited an old acquaintance of his, a man who did little else but sit in a rocking chair, staring into space. The man wasn't ill; he had his wits about him, but he did nothing. He was a bit younger than Kim, but he looked as though he were in his eighties.

The man—I'll call him Jack—watched while Kim did the complex set of stretching exercises he does each day before going out to run. Jack was amazed that Kim, older than he, could do such things. Kim said "try this" and got his friend to bend over with his knees straight and arms extended toward the floor. His hands could reach no more than half way down his legs, but it was a start. Jack was elated. He had given up on his ability to reach his knees, much less approach his toes.

Kim began to visit Jack regularly. He showed him more stretches, and soon Jack began walking on a regular basis. One thing led to another, and a year later Jack was one of the most active members of his retirement community. He exercised regularly, stretching, PaceWalking, and even running. He began to play eighteen holes of golf two to three times a week. He did community volunteer work and showed other older people how to re-activate themselves. And his wife, who had been forced to stay at home to tend to him while he sat in his chair, was free to go back to work doing floral design.

Jack's is a success story, a wonderful example of what exercise can do to renew life in the worn out and run down. For Jack, it was like winding up the spring; had he started exercising earlier in life, particularly with a low-stress exercise like PaceWalking, there would have been little need for the spring to have wound down so much in the first place. And this particular success story, like so many others, started small—in this case, with a single stretch.

Exercise can actually help you *think* better. Believe it or not, aging people who exercise can reason more effectively than those who don't exercise. Aerobic exercise can actually increase blood flow to various parts of the brain. It can increase the speed of nerve messages traveling through the brain as well. That old business of being able to get some of your best thinking done while you exercise seems to have a physiological basis.

That's good news for anyone, of course, but it's *terrific* news for aging people. Loss of mental sharpness is a cliché of aging. If something so simple and accessible as exercise might circumvent this most unfortunate decline, all the more reason for giving it a try.

How Aging People Should Exercise

First, it's important to remember that this is *moderate* exercise we're talking about—no back-breaking regimens here. This is the kind and duration of exercise I've been recommending all the way through this book, a level of exercise virtually anyone can do. In fact, not only will a steady diet of PaceWalking satisfy the needs of aging exercisers, there's no better exercise possible.

The reasons are threefold. First, PaceWalking is effective aerobic exercise and, as we've seen, it's aerobic exercise that hits the primary characteristic of aging and disuse, the deterioration of cardiovascular capability.

Second, PaceWalking offers a complete body workout. Along with aerobic dance, it's the only major aerobic activity to do so.

And third, PaceWalking is perhaps the most gentle and certainly the most accessible aerobic activity. It's also the most attractive to seniors who know they really should exercise but just can't muster up much enthusiasm for it. These people are much more likely to rouse themselves for a good, brisk walk than for a jog around the block. In fact, I shudder to think of elderly people who have not exercised for years suddenly embarking on a rigorous jogging program, for example, or even an overenthusiastic stretching program. That can be dangerous as well as uncomfortable. But there's little that can go wrong in PaceWalking. Do too much of it, or do it with too much gusto, and you may end up worn out and a little sore, but that's about it. The possibility of damage to limbs, joints, and muscles is small compared to most other exercise activities.

But there's no reason, really, to go about PaceWalking or doing any other aerobic activity in the wrong way. It's important to start out gradually in anything, no matter the activity or the age of the person doing it. When it comes to aging people, it's even more important to take it slow. Do too much too soon, and although you may not severely injure yourself, you're certainly not doing yourself much good. In fact, you can actually set yourself back, forcing your body to work just to get to where you started out. And if where you started out wasn't much to begin with, then you've really got a problem.

It's important to start slowly and build up slowly. Here's a way of doing that.

See Your Doctor First

For aging people, a checkup is very important, for obvious reasons. And if you haven't exercised much in the last few years, or if you have any chronic health problems, or if you're taking medication, it's vitally important that you see a doctor first. Any exercise, even the most gentle, involves some risk. That risk is compounded if you have medical problems to begin with. Let your doctor advise you as to whether exercise might be appropriate for you.

But be careful. Like much of the rest of our society, at least until very recently, doctors sometimes underestimate the value of exercise for older adults or overemphasize its risks. And some doctors aren't as knowledgeable when it comes to the needs and problems of older people as they are for younger folks. Very few medical schools, even in these comparatively enlightened times, spend any time at all teaching their students and residents about the positive impact that exercise can have on the lives of their patients, let alone how doctors can educate their patients about exercise. And years ago, when many of today's practitioners were trained, there were no schools teaching anything about the benefits of exercise—if for no other reason than that the benefits were not understood. So if your doctor tells you not to exercise, there may be very good reasons why, but if you're not convinced, it can't hurt to get a second opinion. As I know only too well, doctors are mortal and therefore fallible.

Warm Up First

The older you are, the more important it is to prepare your body for exercise, especially if you haven't done much of it lately. Happily, PaceWalking provides its own built-in warm up. If you start out walking slowly, then build up to the aerobic range, you will have automatically warmed your muscles.

Stretch Before Exercising

I always stretch before starting out. Other people stretch during or after their workout, or not at all. There's certainly no agreement on this point. But I would say that for older people, especially those who haven't exercised for a very long time, gentle stretching before embarking on a workout program can be very beneficial.

Exercise Consistently and Regularly

No aerobic exercise program can be effective if it's done only once in a while. And as important as that credo is for younger people, it's especially important for seniors. For as we age, we fall out of condition more rapidly than in our younger days. If you miss too many days, whether from neglect or illness, it's all that much harder to get back to where you were. By following the schedules to come, if only in general approach rather than to the letter, you'll be right on target.

On the other hand, don't think you have to push on even if you're sick. Take time off; but when you feel better, remember you have to start back at a lower level than you were when you stopped. Then work back up.

Know Your Aerobic Heart Rate

The aerobic heart rate range for seniors may be somewhat lower than that for younger people (see the table on the minimum aerobic heart rate by age on page 27). Remember, the aerobic range is determined by subtracting your age from 220 and then taking 70 to 85 percent of that (on page 28 I explain how to take your pulse). So for a forty-year-old, the aerobic range is between approximately 125 and 155 beats per minute. Keep your heart rate in that range for at least twenty minutes three times a week, and you'll realize aerobic benefits.

But seniors tend to realize the same gains at a lower rate—that is, older people don't need to exercise quite so strenuously to benefit from their activities. For some aging people, 60 to 75 percent of maximum heart rate may be good enough. For example, let's apply the aerobic formula to a person of seventy-five. Anywhere from approximately 90 to 110 beats per minute may well afford an aerobic workout. In the beginning, at least, if you can keep your heart rate in that range, you'll be doing just fine. As you improve your level of aerobic fitness, you may want to raise your minimum target heart rate to the 70 percent level, but there's no need to do so. Be your own expert in this case; if you feel comfortable at the lower level, stick with it. It's probably the right one for you.

At the same time, however, be careful at the higher end of the aerobic heart rate scale. If you sense your heart beating really fast—uncomfortably fast—stop PaceWalking and take your pulse. If it's above the upper limit of the range for your age, don't start PaceWalking again. Walk slowly until your heart rate comes down. Then start PaceWalking again, this time at a reduced speed. (If your heart rate often has a tendency to shoot up, consult your doctor. If you are on a medication that can affect heart rate, like a beta-blocker such as lopressor or tenormin, consult a knowledgeable physician about what the appropriate heart rate range is for you.)

Know Your Limits

If you hurt after exercising and the pain just won't go away, or if you don't sleep well, or are tired all the time, you're probably doing too much. On the other hand, if you find you just can't get your heart rate up to the aerobic range of at least 60 percent of maximum, don't despair. All you can give is your best effort. (One way to deal with a reduced heart rate is simply to exercise more. Twenty-five minutes of 50 percent of maximum heart rate or thirty minutes of 40 percent of maximum may afford aging people worthwhile aerobic benefits.) Listen to your body. Don't do things that make you feel worse rather than better. The idea of all of this exercise business is that it be fun and beneficial at the same time.

Cool Down after Exercising

It's not a good idea to abruptly stop exercising. When you're active, effective circulation of the blood depends on muscle movement as well as the pumping action of the heart. If you stop abruptly, that muscle movement stops, and the heart finds itself in the position of suddenly having to do more of the work. At the same time, if it finds its own blood supply curtailed, which can happen because of the muscles' sudden relaxation, you can find yourself in real trouble. So walk a bit beyond your aerobic workout. Don't PaceWalk. Just keep moving until your cardiovascular system has a chance to stabilize. A couple of minutes will most likely do it. Then cool down a bit before taking a hot shower or Jacuzzi or sauna.

Two more things. For all its benefits, exercise is not a cure-all. It can slow down and even reverse some of the ravages of age, yes; but it won't keep you young forever. Despite all I've said in this chapter, the best way to approach exercise is by not expecting too much from it. Do it because you like it; that's the best reason. Consider any benefits—and there almost certainly will be benefits—as frosting on the cake. Then you won't be disappointed if the results are not as dramatic or widespread as you had expected.

And any exercise involves risk. No matter how little, there's still some risk. It may be that for some people the risk outweighs the benefit—that's for you, and perhaps your doctor, to decide.

Exercise isn't for everyone. One thing I can say with great confidence and enthusiasm, however, is that one way or another, in one guise or another, it most assuredly is for most people. The thing is to find the approach that works for you.

PaceWalking for Older People— The Program

Stretching

Gentle stretching should be a part of every older person's workout, especially if you haven't exercised for some time. If you get into a regular program, and if you're feeling pretty good, with no lingering aches and pains, you may want to reduce the amount of stretching. But some stretching should be a part of every workout.

When muscles age they become more susceptible to damage; stretching helps to mitigate this risk.

I recommend the following stretches in particular, all of which I discussed in chapter 3; turn there for detailed descriptions and illustrations of how to do the stretches, always remembering that they should be done gently and slowly. Gradually pull the muscles to the point where you feel pressure but not pain. If it hurts to do the stretch, stop at the point at which the pain shows up. In time you'll become more flexible, and you'll be able to do more.

Reach for the Sky Stretch

As you can see, I've focused on stretches that loosen up and strengthen the body. You may want to add leg stretches as well, but the body stretches are the most important to begin with.

Back and spine twist, page 55
Back and spine stretch, page 56
Curl-ups, page 58
Arm rotations, page 59

And here's one more. Let's call it Reach for the Sky.

Stand with your feet comfortably apart. Reach up with your arms as far as you can. Breathe easily, hold for no more than ten seconds, and then bring your arms slowly back down to your sides. This movement stretches your entire upper torso—you can feel it—as well as your arms. It should feel good. You can easily repeat the motion one or two times.

Introductory Program for the Older Person

The first four weeks of this program are the same as the first four weeks of the Introductory Program in chapter 4. This period *does not* introduce aerobic exercise. Its purpose is to introduce you to the idea of exercising on a regular basis, setting up a program, and sticking to it.

That's the key. Once exercise becomes a regular part of your life, two things happen: You begin to realize benefits from it and you become psychologically committed to it. In this case, you're much more likely to stick with it than if you do it now and then. It really is a chicken-or-egg situation. You won't realize physical and mental benefits unless you exercise regularly, but you need to feel and see those benefits in order to cement your commitment to regular exercise.

For older people, however, three things mitigate what I've just said. The first is common to anyone who works out regularly, especially those who PaceWalk: Exercising is fun. You may find that

Introductory Program for the
Older Person
(Times in Minutes)

Week	M	T	W	Th	F	S	S	Total	
1	Off	10	Off	10	Off	Off	10	30	Ordinary
2	Off	10	Off	10	Off	Off	10	30	Walking
3	Off	20	Off	20	Off	Off	20	60	Ordinary
4	Off	20	Off	20	Off	Off	20	60	Walking
5	Off	10	Off	10	Off	Off	10	30	Fast
6	Off	10	Off	10	Off	Off	20	40	Walking
7	Off	20	Off	20	Off	Off	20	60	Fast
8	Off	20	Off	20	Off	Off	20	60	Walking
9	Off	10	Off	10	Off	Off	10	30	PaceWalking
10	Off	10	Off	10	Off	Off	20	40	
11	Off	20	Off	20	Off	Off	20	60	PaceWalking
12	Off	20	Off	20	Off	Off	20	60	
13	Off	30	Off	30	Off	Off	30	90	PaccWalking

Average: 50 minutes per week for thirteen weeks

you'll be inclined to stick with it no matter how quickly the benefits may come. The doing itself is enjoyable.

The second aspect is that for older people perceptible benefits may come more quickly than they do for younger people, especially if you've been inactive for a long time. It's like anything—first strides may be the hardest, but they also bring the most spectacular changes.

And the third is that exercising regularly provides a feeling of control over your life. *This*, at least, is something you can do and do consistently—time, age, and decline be damned. One of the problems of aging is the sense of helplessness it sometimes brings. Time is getting away from you. Death is that much closer. The ages that appear in the obituary column creep ever closer to your own and then imperceptibly fall below. It becomes harder to concentrate, and memory is something that deserts you for recent events, but grows for early experiences. And for retired people there is the problem of what to do with all that time. Do nothing, and time—dead time—takes over.

A regular exercise program serves to put you back in control, at least partially. You're no longer waiting passively to see what life will deal you—you're doing something about it. If there were no other benefits to exercising, that feeling itself would make it worth doing. The benefits to come are just the frosting on the cake.

The next four weeks of the program are the fast walking stage. This is nothing fancy—no more than brisk walking using your own gait. Now's the time to become thoroughly comfortable with the regular, rhythmic arm swing of ordinary walking. The pattern of opposite arm forward with each stride should become second nature. Believe it or not, there are people who have trouble coordinating this movement—including, on occasion, yours truly. And for older people, who may have not done much extended walking in quite some time, the seemingly simplest of movements, such as this one, can be a real handful.

These first eight weeks of workouts are not intended to be aerobic, although for some they may be. They're concerned primarily with getting you into a pattern of regular exercise and with putting back into use muscles that may have been unused for a long period of time.

PaceWalking begins with week nine. Now's the time to add the vigorous arm swing I described in chapter 3. The sessions are relatively easy—just ten minutes at a time. But the primary goal of weeks nine and ten is still not aerobic exercise per se. It's getting used to the gait and continuing to establish regularity.

Now you may not want to proceed this slowly. If you've a mind to and your body feels up to it, you can move more quickly through the program. But this pace will accommodate just about any older person and, most important, will not cause problems.

The PaceWalking proceeds at a modest clip through the last four weeks. During week eleven you'll do your first "aerobic minimum" week—three twenty-minute sessions. And by week thirteen you'll be ready to do three thirty-minute sessions, for a grand total of ninety minutes of PaceWalking for the week.

Again, concentrate on keeping to the schedule all the way through the thirteen weeks. It's important to establish a regular rhythm of PaceWalking and the habit of exercising regularly. Do so, and I anticipate most older people will start perceiving benefits within the first four weeks. By the time you start actually PaceWalking, you ought to be feeling pretty darn good about yourself.

Developmental Program for the Older Person

The Developmental Program for the older person averages 90 minutes per week for twelve weeks (remember, the first week of each program after the Introductory one is *off*). That compares with 120 minutes per week for the comparable program in chapter 4. Now you'll be PaceWalking exclusively, and by week six you'll be doing so four times a week, with back-to-back workouts on the weekends. The peak occurs during week eleven, when you'll PaceWalk 130 minutes, with 80 of those minutes during your weekend sessions. Then, as always in these programs, the time drops back down for a while.

You may want to go through the thirteen weeks of this program and move directly to the (generic) Developmental Program described in chapter 4; that's a reasonable next step. Or you may want to repeat the last six weeks of this program before going on. Or you may not wish to go on at all, preferring to stick at the level of the last weeks of this program. The choice is yours. By this time you're an experienced PaceWalker and should know better than anyone else your limits and possibilities.

And by now you should be feeling much, much better than

Developmental Program for the
Older Person
(Times in Minutes)

Week	M	T	W	Th	F	S	S	Total
1	Off	Off	Off	Off	Off	Off	Off	Off
2	Off	20	Off	20	Off	Off	20	60
3	Off	20	Off	20	Off	Off	20	60
4	Off	20	Off	20	Off	Off	30	70
5	Off	20	Off	30	Off	Off	30	80
6	Off	20	Off	20	Off	20	20	80
7	Off	20	Off	20	Off	20	30	90
8	Off	20	Off	20	Off	30	20	90
9	Off	30	Off	20	Off	30	30	110
10	Off	20	Off	30	Off	30	40	120
11	Off	30	Off	20	Off	30	50	130
12	Off	20	Off	20	Off	30	30	100
13	Off	20	Off	20	Off	20	30	90

you have in ages. In fact, it may be interesting for you to go back over some of the benefits of aerobic exercise that I discussed earlier in this chapter. Now that you're *feeling* them, it may be helpful to be reminded of what's going on inside.

For many older people, the experience of exercising is an immensely gratifying one. Perhaps you're one of those people. If so, I can only say *Bravo!* And welcome to the community of exercisers.

CHAPTER 6

PaceWalking and Pregnancy

One of the disappointments of modern medicine has been its attitude toward pregnant women. Not toward pregnancy; that's not what I mean. We've learned a great deal about pregnancy and have made great strides in treating many of the problems of pregnancy. No, I mean our attitude toward healthy women who are pregnant. It seems that many doctors—most of whom are men, of course—have tended to regard pregnant women as patients with an illness and their state of pregnancy as a problem to be treated rather than as a natural condition to be supported and fortified. A great deal of attention has been paid to difficult pregnancies and the actual process of giving birth—monitoring the fetus, administering labor-inducing and pain-killing drugs, delivering and caring for premature infants, virtually eliminating the threat of Rh Negative disease, that kind of thing, all of which is undeniably important. Prenatal care in terms of following the development of the fetus, protecting the mother against illness and toxic exposures, providing advice on nutrition, has all improved. But relatively little thought has been given to how to help healthy pregnant women become healthier and more fit, so as to experience a healthier birth and postdelivery period.

Nowhere has that shortcoming been more glaring than in the area of exercise for pregnant women. Indeed, until recently medical recommendations for exercise during pregnancy have been based on arbitrary guesswork rather than scientific investigation. With a few laudable exceptions, the medical profession has told pregnant women that when it comes to exercise, they are on their own, and they're probably better off doing nothing.

All that is beginning to change, and change for the better. In May of 1985 the American College of Obstetricians and Gynecologists (ACOG) introduced guidelines for exercise during pregnancy, the culmination of a year's study by an eight-member panel. Since then more research has been done, and a number of articles and a few books have been written on the subject. We now know far more than we ever have, but—just between you and me—it's not all that much. We're just at the beginning of this particular road.

So this chapter will review what we do know about exercise during pregnancy and how PaceWalking fits in. As you read, keep a couple of things in mind. The first is that, as with any kind of exercise for any kind of people, common sense is a pretty good indicator no matter the situation. If in doubt, *listen* to your body. Trust how you *feel*. If exercise makes you feel better, it's probably doing good things for you—if not, probably not. Remember, when it comes to PaceWalking at least, particularly during pregnancy, pain is *not* gain. Don't exercise so that you hurt. Exercise so that you feel better.

The second caution is this: Before beginning or continuing any exercise program, pregnant women should consult their doctors. That's good advice in the best of situations; it's especially important if there's a possibility that you may fall into that small group that doctors like to label "high risk." Here's what to look out for:

1. Active heart disease
2. Thrombophlebitis (an infection of veins in the legs)
3. Recent pulmonary embolus (blood clot in the lungs)
4. Active infectious disease
5. High blood pressure
6. Problems with the immune system
7. Thyroid disease
8. Diabetes
9. Anemia
10. Being exessively over- or underweight
11. No prenatal care
12. Known fetal illness
13. Abnormal fetal position in the womb during the last trimester
14. At risk for premature labor
15. Two or more fetuses in the womb
16. Any bleeding from the vagina or signs of weakness of the cervix
17. Abnormally large or small fetus

If any of these conditions describes your pregnancy, or if you even suspect you have one of them, you should consult your doctor before starting an exercise program. Realize, however, that even if you do fall into the high-risk group, you may still be able to exercise. In fact, exercise can help manage many of the conditions on this list. You simply have to be careful.

Whether or not you fall into the high-risk group, if your doctor says no to exercise but your body tells you yes, consider getting another opinion. Even the best doctors can be overcautious or biased against exercise. You certainly want to work with your doctor, but at the same time you want to be sure your doctor is interested in working with you.

Use common sense and consult your physician. I can suggest some possible approaches, but it's up to you and your physician to rework them so that they'll be right for you.

Setting Goals for Exercising During Pregnancy

As you know by now, for anyone planning an exercise program the most important step is to set your goals. Just what is it that you want to get out of exercise? The question is no less important for women who have been regular exercisers and want to continue through their pregnancy than it is for pregnant women who plan to begin exercising for the first time. Are you already aerobically fit and simply want to maintain that level? Are you exercising to help control your weight gain during pregnancy? Are you exercising to keep up your figure—literally as well as figuratively? Or do you simply want to *feel* good, and feel good *about* yourself?

Whatever your goals, they should reflect what *you* want for yourself, not what someone else may think is best for you. They should fit into your life-style and your daily schedule. They should be consistent with your exercise history. Trust yourself. Remember, an exercise approach that *feels* right for you and your baby most likely *is* right. With your doctor's help, you should go ahead and follow through.

A Woman's Body During Pregnancy

What happens to a woman's body during pregnancy? Lots. As the body gears up to become, in effect, a baby factory, the physiological processes that previously benefited the woman alone now turn toward producing a healthy baby. With regard to exercising, much of the energy that used to propel you along the track, or through the water, or in the workout studio now becomes rerouted to fuel the developing life inside you. That can be a shock to any woman and particularly to an active, fit woman. If you've been used to a certain level of exercise, and for no apparent reason—nothing that *shows*, anyhow—that level suddenly becomes unattainable, you may well wonder just what the heck's going on.

For example, the first three months of pregnancy are sometimes accompanied by loss of appetite and the nausea of morning sickness, with a resulting loss of vitality. You may not feel like exercising—such is the experience of many women. And even if you're one of that fortunate group of pregnant women who sails through the first trimester without being plagued by the greenies, you'll most likely find that you tire more easily than before and that your performance level drops accordingly.

It's in the second and third trimesters that your pregnancy becomes obvious to others. If during the first three months it sapped energy and made you forget what it was like to consistently feel good through an entire day, now it introduces interesting changes in your body's proportions, your center of gravity, and your weight. You may no longer feel green in the morning, and your appetite may have returned and then some, but now you're noticing flesh where there was none before, and bulges appear in places that used to be flat. Your weight may increase dramatically. Now's when breasts begin to swell and become heavier, tending to pull your shoulders and therefore your neck and head forward, often producing the slouch associated with the advanced stages of pregnancy. And the enlarging uterus stretches the stomach muscles and correspondingly shortens the lower back muscles, bringing about a swayback posture. Together, these developments cause your center of gravity to change—from day to day, it may seem—as your pregnancy progresses. After a while you may wonder whose body you're exercising in, anyhow.

There are other, more subtle changes as well. For example, hormone levels change during pregnancy. The secretion of hormones such as estrogen, progesterone, and elastin, which are necessary to prolong and promote pregnancy, have the effect of softening connective tisue. Connective tissue does just what its name suggests: It *connects* other, more specialized tissue—bone to bone, for example, or muscle to bone. As you might expect, connective tissue often shows up in joints. Cartilage, ligaments, and tendons are all types of connective tissue. When these tissues soften as a result of the change in hormone levels, the joints that they bind together become looser, less stable, more susceptible to injury.

During pregnancy, the volume of blood in your body increases, and your heart tends to work harder than usual to accommodate the augmented blood flow. More work demands more oxygen, but when you're pregnant that oxygen is actually harder to come by. The reason has to do with the growing uterus. Because it not only expands out and downward, causing your stomach muscles to stretch, but upwards as well, it eventually displaces the organs directly above it. That displacement crowds the space normally reserved for the lungs, reducing the lungs' ability to expand when you take a deep breath. And reduced lung capacity reduces the amount of oxygen a pregnant woman is able to breathe in.

This increased volume of blood means that you'll feel your heart beating faster, at rest as well as during activity, as it works to pump that extra blood through your body. You'll experience the reduced lung capacity as a tendency to become short of breath. These two tendencies do not complement each other. They demand special vigilance when it comes to exercise.

Your ankles and legs tend to swell, too, as your body retains fluid during pregnancy. Likewise, blood vessels tend to enlarge. Pregnancy is a time of high risk for varicose veins. Thus pregnant women sometimes wear firm stockings and experience the beneficial effects of elevating their legs at the end of the day.

Exercise and Pregnancy

There's no doubt about the preceding information. As for what exercise can do to help you deal with it, however, there is doubt. Not that exercise before, during, and after pregnancy isn't good for you—it is. Most people would certainly agree with that. Many women report that if nothing else, exercise helps them feel positive about themselves and their pregnancy. It can help to avoid excessive weight gain. Aerobic exercise can help women handle the routines of daily life with less fatigue and discomfort. It may not make labor and birth any easier but, offering the assurance that she's fit and healthy, it may increase a woman's confidence. The recuperation time immediately after giving birth may be lessened because of exercise, and the lasting return of strength and endurance is quicker.

The difficulty comes with regard to what kind of exercise and how much. This is the area in which many physicians feel inadequate to advise. It's a topic about which there's lots of disagreement. And it's a subject in which women have often had to rely on their own—largely uninformed—common sense. There simply hasn't been much research or investigation done.

The American College of Obstetricians and Gynecologists' 1985 Guidelines for Exercise During Pregnancy and Postpartum was the first major step in illuminating this shadowy area. Even though these recommendations haven't satisfied everyone, it's worth quoting them in full.

Pregnancy and Postpartum

1. Regular exercise (at least three times per week) is preferable to intermittent activity. Competitive activities should be discouraged.
2. Vigorous exercise should not be performed in hot, humid weather or during a period of febrile [fever-related] illness.
3. Ballistic movements (jerky, bouncy motions) should be avoided. Exercise should be done on a wooden floor or a tightly carpeted surface to reduce shock and provide a sure footing.
4. Deep flexion or extension of joints should be avoided because of connective tissue laxity [the softening of connective tissue I mentioned earlier]. Activities that require jumping, jarring motions, or rapid changes in direction should be avoided because of joint instability.
5. Vigorous exercise should be preceded by a five-minute period of muscle warm-up. This can be accomplished by slow walking or stationary cycling with low resistance.
6. Vigorous exercise should be followed by a period of gradually declining activity that includes gentle stationary stretching. Because connective tissue laxity increases the risk of joint injury, stretches should not be taken to the point of maximum resistance.
7. Heart rate should be measured at times of peak activity. Target heart rates and limits established in consultation with the physician should not be exceeded.
8. Care should be taken to rise gradually from the floor to avoid orthostatic hypotension [sudden drop in blood pressure]. Some form of activity involving the legs should be continued for a brief period.

9. Liquids should be taken liberally before and after exercise to prevent dehydration. If necessary, activity should be interrupted to replenish fluids.
10. Women who have led sedentary life-styles should begin with physical activity of very low intensity and advance activity levels very gradually.
11. Activity should be stopped and the physician consulted if any unusual symptoms appear.

Pregnancy Only

1. Maternal heart rate should not exceed 140 beats/min.
2. Strenuous activities should not exceed 15 minutes duration.
3. No exercise should be performed in the supine [lying on your back] position after the fourth month of gestation is completed.
4. Exercises that employ the Valsalva maneuver [increasing abdominal pressure, as in pushing down during birth] should be avoided.
5. Calorie intake should be adequate to meet not only the extra energy needs of pregnancy, but also the exercise performed.
6. Maternal core temperature should not exceed 38 degrees C [100.4 degrees F].

Well, except for number 4 in the first part of the guidelines (about avoiding deep flexion and extension of joints due to the softening of connective tissue—a good idea for obvious reasons), the general section offers nothing new for the exerciser. Anyone who's ever worked out at all will recognize these suggestions; those who haven't might well see them as little more than good common sense. And of course that's the point. Exercise should be approached with good common sense, pregnant or not. In this case, of course, it's particularly important to be smart about yourself—or, in the case of pregnant women, your*selves*. That, too, is the point.

It's the second part of the guidelines, the section for pregnancy only, that presents a significant departure from the approach women who exercise might tend to take on their own. And it is these guidelines about which there is some controversy. Some authorities, such as the sports gynecologist Mona Shangold, M.D., consider them too restrictive and conservative to be applied to all women. They believe in the individualized approach.

I tend to agree with them. I also think that the ACOG guidelines do provide a very good starting point, especially for pregnant women who have exercised little or not at all. But if you're already fit, and you don't have a high-risk pregnancy, you may be able to do much more than the guidelines suggest. The experience of world-class runners Joan Benoit Samuelson and Mary Decker Slaney, both of whom ran during their pregnancies, argues for the individualized approach.

The guidelines recommend that a pregnant woman's heart rate not exceed 140 beats per minute. Although that figure exceeds the minimum aerobic heart rate for anyone twenty years and older (see the minimum aerobic heart rate table on page 27), it doesn't do so by much, at least not for younger exercisers, and many people may be used to pushing their heart rate higher than the bare minimum. The question is, why should pregnant women who exercise take pains to keep their heart rate at the low end of the aerobic range?

The answer involves the fact, discussed earlier, that a pregnant woman's heart must work especially hard to pump an increased volume of blood. Your heart is beating faster than usual even before you exercise. When you exercise, therefore, and push your heart rate higher, your heart has less in reserve. It can be dangerous to push a heart too close to its maximum in the most congenial of situations. During pregnancy, when your heart must work hard even in relatively unstressed moments, the danger is intensified. Thus the recommendation is a maximum of 140 beats per minute.

The recommendation is based on research suggesting that strenuous exercise may cause problems in a developing fetus. One study reports that a fetus's heart rate tends to stay elevated long after the mother finishes exercising. Although the tendency may not mean much for a healthy fetus, one with problems might be harmed. That's why it is important to be certain that you and your fetus are healthy before taking on anything too strenuous. But if you are already well trained and used to exercise, and you don't have a high-risk pregnancy, it's probably all right to exceed the 140-beats-per-minute figure.

As for the suggested time limit of fifteen minutes per session, there is considerable controversy. For the sedentary or minimally trained woman, it may be a good idea to stick with the fifteen-minute limit until you feel comfortable PaceWalking. Then you should be able to go safely to twenty minutes. But for the well-trained pregnant woman, fifteen minutes seems an arbitrary number right from the start—unless you're in the high-risk group. So if your pregnancy is normal and you're feeling good, there is no reason why you cannot go longer than fifteen or even twenty minutes. Most of the training programs at the end of the chapter are for twenty minutes; you have to use your discretion and common sense in deciding what's best for you.

Guideline number 3, which warns against exercising while flat on your back, is a precaution aimed at avoiding a loss in blood pressure. There's evidence that a supine position can bring about a sudden loss of blood pressure early in pregnancy; later on it can cause the enlarged uterus to press against the aorta, reducing its own blood supply. Guideline number 4, a suggestion to avoid movements similar to those employed to push the baby out of the birth canal, is self-explanatory. Pushing is supremely useful and necessary during birth; it should be avoided otherwise.

And number 5, the admonition to eat well, is likewise self-evident. You're not only eating for two, you also need to eat to provide the extra energy that exercise requires.

The last recommendation, that concerning "maternal core temperature," may seem like something out of *The China Syn-*

drome, but it's very important. If your internal temperature—the temperature inside your womb—rises above 100.4 degrees Farenheit, there is risk of damage to the fetus, especially during the first trimester. Not to worry, however. Most people's temperature-regulating mechanisms are very good. It's just a good idea to take a few precautions.

First, especially during your first trimester, don't exercise out-of-doors in hot weather. Do no more than twenty minutes if the temperature is above 75 degrees, and do nothing at all if it's hotter than 85 degrees.

Second, if you do exercise in a hot climate, wear as little clothing as possible. If you must cover up for the sake of modesty, then it might be a good idea to exercise indoors in an air-conditioned room.

Third, regardless of where you exercise and how much you do, if you feel yourself getting hot, slow down or stop.

Fourth, make sure you drink enough water. Stay well hydrated at all times. The body uses water, in the form of perspiration, to maintain normal body temperature. If you run out of water, your core temperature can rise rapidly.

So where does all that leave us? In a nutshell, the ACOG recommends that pregnant women exercise regularly, at least three times a week, that no exercise should push the heart rate much beyond the minimum aerobic range, that pregnant women should warm up and warm down carefully, that nonexercisers should begin gradually, and that pregnant women should eat and drink intelligently to avoid dehydration and energy depletion. I'll tell you what all that suggests to me: PaceWalking is the ideal aerobic exercise for the pregnant woman.

PaceWalking and Pregnancy

For pregnant women there's no better aerobic exercise than PaceWalking—no safer aerobic exercise, no milder aerobic exercise, no more enjoyable aerobic exercise.

Of course it doesn't take much insight to make that statement. The reasons should be obvious to anyone. I'm certainly not the first to espouse walking as a suitable activity for pregnant women. Even in the days when pregnant women were advised to do little but rest for nine months, doctors often suggested walking as the one exercise that was both safe and good for you. Nothing has changed in that regard. Here's why.

• Walking puts little stress on bones and joints, which, as we've seen, is particularly important during pregnancy when joints tend to loosen up. It avoids bouncing and quick, jerky movements, which are unavoidable in such activities as running, aerobic dance, and tennis, for example, but may be risky as well as uncomfortable for pregnant women.

• As compared to other aerobic activities, walking doesn't so readily make you short of breath. As we've seen, pregnant women have less oxygen reserve to call upon. Walking, the gentlest of aerobic activities, doesn't demand that you deplete those reserves. It can provide a controlled aerobic workout. You can easily work out at a low aerobic intensity—for example, with your heart rate in the 125 to 140 beats per minute range.

• Walking strengthens the muscles in the back and buttocks, thereby helping to relieve or prevent back pain caused by the pregnant woman's tendency to overarch her back. The swayback posture may be unavoidable during pregnancy, but walking helps to keep it to a minimum.

• Walking increases circulation in the extremities, thereby helping to avoid swelling in the legs and ankles. In contrast to an injury, say, a sprained ankle, in which swelling is caused by torn blood vessels emptying into the area, swelling during pregnancy is the result of the tendency to retain fluids—the condition is called edema. Increased blood circulation helps to channel that fluid away.

• Walking helps avoid varicose veins. Walking exercises the

muscles in the legs, which, by contracting, in turn contract blood vessels in the area. Varicose veins are nothing more than enlarged, distended blood vessels. By contracting the blood vessels and keeping circulation strong, walking helps to avoid the problem. It doesn't replace elevating your legs, but it can augment its benefits.

• Walking is at once the easiest, safest, and most natural of exercise activities. It requires little training and coordination. During pregnancy, when your center of gravity seems to change almost daily and the simplest of movements can take on unexpected difficulty, walking offers little physical difficulty and little risk of falling. Other than being on your feet to walk at all, which itself can be something of a trial in the latter stages of pregnancy, walking is without any major disadvantages. You can trust it as an effective, *doable* exercise.

How to PaceWalk During Pregnancy

A word to the wise: Any exercising you do *during* pregnancy will benefit you most if you're already in the habit of exercising *before* pregnancy. One of the tenets of any beneficial aerobic exercise program, and certainly of the approach to PaceWalking that I've been building throughout this book, is that consistency and regularity are absolutely necessary if you're to realize aerobic benefits from your exercise. The more healthy and fit you are when you become pregnant, the more healthy and fit you'll be through your pregnancy and afterwards. And what you do before you're pregnant will to a large extent determine what you're able to do during pregnancy. So if you're new to exercise, and you're reading this chapter with an eye to getting pregnant, start with one of the PaceWalking programs offered in chapter 4.

If you're already accustomed to exercise, it may be a bit of a surprise to discover that you just can't keep up your usual level, or type, of activity when you're pregnant. Runners may find that as their weight increases and center of gravity changes, running can become laborious indeed. Cyclists will most likely have a tough time getting and remaining on a bike; bike seats can be awfully hard and uncomfortable for a pregnant body. Aerobic dancers may find the bouncing and bending uncomfortable, especially as they grow larger. Swimmers? Well, swimming rivals walking as a particularly congenial exercise for pregnant women. The escape from gravity when you slide into the buoyant water can be a wonderful relief. The problem is that often women aren't comfortable displaying a pregnant body in a swimsuit (an attitude that may be changing, however. It's no longer unheard of for dedicated swimmers to notice gloriously pregnant bodies in two-piece bathing suits swimming laps right alongside them). And even walkers themselves will have to modify their duration and pace as pregnancy proceeds.

For all these women, PaceWalking is probably the ideal exercise during pregnancy. Certainly it is for women who have never exercised before. For runners, it can afford the same aerobic benefits without the risks and discomfort. The same goes for cyclists, swimmers, and aerobic dancers. And already-practicing Pace-Walkers can sail right through by taking a less strenuous tack.

How do you go about it? First, realize that pregnancy is like nothing you've experienced before (unless you've been pregnant before, of course, but even then women report that no two pregnancies are alike). For example, as I've noted above, it's particularly important not to become dehydrated. One recommendation is that in warm weather you drink eight to twelve ounces of cool fluid— *not* soft drinks—for every ten to fifteen minutes of PaceWalking. You'll quickly become aware of your own needs, but the important thing is that you shouldn't wait until you become thirsty. You could've already lost a great deal of fluid by then. (All of which brings up one of the characteristic features of pregnancy: the need to urinate frequently. The important thing here is that you not stint on drinking fluids to avoid visiting a rest room so often. Stay well hydrated; that's much more important than the occasional inconvenience.)

Adequately support your burgeoning body. Particularly in the later stages of your pregnancy, as your breasts enlarge and you put on weight, wear a firm, supportive bra. Some women recommend wearing two. And a good pair of shoes is also important, perhaps even more so. Pregnancy forces your feet to bear more weight, and because the distribution of that weight changes, weak areas of your feet that aren't used to supporting weight may become overburdened. Your feet may start to ache more frequently and with less provocation than before.

Any good running or walking shoes will probably do. (See chapter 3 for a discussion of what to look for in shoes.) They should have a broad-based heel for support. By the way, pregnancy is no time to wear shoes with flat soles, such as baseball or soccer shoes, or precarious heels, a description that applies to any number of dress shoes. You want your shoes to provide as much support and protection as possible.

It's probably not a good idea to PaceWalk when you're not feeling well, especially if you have a fever. Also, as I suggested before, be careful of exercising in hot and humid weather. Neither your temperature nor your heart rate should rise above the limits already suggested. Heat, whether from without or within, affects both.

Because it's important not to push your heart rate to too high a level, check it every few minutes, certainly more often than you did before you were pregnant. Stay on top of your heart rate. If it's climbing too high, stop until you have it under control once again.

Finally, if you develop any of the following symptoms, *stop PaceWalking and see a doctor:*

> pain in any area of the body
> leg cramps
> uterine cramps or bleeding
> severe shortness of breath
> dizziness or extreme fatigue
> extremely rapid heart rate

heart palpitations or irregularities
decreased fetal movement
anything else unusual

No matter what the benefits of exercise may be, they are not worth taking a chance with your health. If in doubt—any doubt about *anything* having to do with your pregnancy—see your doctor.

The PaceWalking Program for Pregnant Women

What follows is a suggestion as to how to go about PaceWalking during pregnancy. I want to emphasize *suggestion*. There just hasn't been enough work done in this area for anyone to be able to recommend with absolute certainty. Besides, every pregnant woman is different and comes to her pregnancy with a different exercise experience. Treat the schedule that follows as a basis from which you, with the help of your doctor, can devise your own workout program.

Introductory Program for the Pregnant PaceWalker

The Introductory Program offers a safe, easy introduction to PaceWalking. If you've never exercised before, or have only exercised sporadically, this is the program for you. It'll guide you gently into the world of aerobic exercise.

Week	M	T	W	Th	F	S	S	Total	
1	Off	10	Off	10	Off	Off	10	30	Ordinary
2	Off	10	Off	10	Off	Off	10	30	Walking
3	Off	10	Off	15	Off	Off	20	45	Ordinary
4	Off	10	Off	15	Off	Off	20	45	Walking
5	Off	10	Off	10	Off	Off	10	30	Fast
6	Off	10	Off	10	Off	Off	10	30	Walking
7	Off	15	Off	15	Off	Off	20	50	Fast
8	Off	15	Off	15	Off	Off	20	50	Walking
9	Off	10	Off	10	Off	Off	15	35	PaceWalking
10	Off	15	Off	15	Off	Off	20	50	
11	Off	15	Off	15	Off	Off	20	50	PaceWalking
12	Off	20	Off	20	Off	Off	20	60	
13	Off	20	Off	20	Off	Off	20	60	PaceWalking

Maintenance Program for the Pregnant PaceWalker

If you're already used to exercising, then the Maintenance Program might be the place to start. In fact, if you're already exercising regularly and your pregnancy is proceeding normally and healthily, you might want to stick to weeks nine to thirteen of the Maintenance Program. You might even feel like increasing your workout. As it stands, those workouts are the aerobic equivalent of running ten to twelve miles per week.

And experienced aerobic athletes who are already exercising three hours per week (the equivalent of fifteen to twenty miles per week of running) may want to do more than is suggested in these programs. If so, consult the Maintenance and Maintenance Plus programs in chapter 4.

The bywords here are *flexibility* and *common sense*. Feel free to use these programs in ways that best suit you. Just listen to your body. If you experience pain you've not had before or feel strange in any way, stop and consult your doctor. You may have to start back at a lower level than before. Be aware of the intensity of your workouts as well; don't drive your heart rate up too high. Be careful not to work out when it's especially hot or humid. And don't become dehydrated. If you go out for over forty minutes, say, plan to stop for a drink along the way or—better yet—take a water bottle with you.

The underlying principles here, as everywhere in this book, are consistency and regularity. Your pregnancy may curtail the intensity and duration of your exercise, but it needn't affect your ability to get out there regularly and exercise for a consistent period of time. That way you'll realize aerobic benefits and increase your level of health and fitness during pregnancy.

Maintenance Program for the Pregnant PaceWalker (Times in Minutes)

Week	M	T	W	Th	F	S	S	Total
1	Off	15	Off	15	Off	Off	15	45
2	Off	15	Off	15	Off	Off	15	45
3	Off	15	Off	15	Off	Off	20	50
4	Off	15	Off	15	Off	Off	20	50
5	Off	20	Off	20	Off	Off	20	60
6	Off	20	Off	20	Off	Off	20	60
7	Off	20	Off	20	Off	Off	30	70
8	Off	20	Off	20	Off	Off	30	70
9	Off	20	Off	20	Off	20	30	90
10	Off	20	Off	30	Off	20	30	100
11	Off	20	Off	30	Off	20	30	100
12	Off	20	Off	30	Off	20	40	110
13	Off	20	Off	30	Off	20	40	110

A Final Word

In this chapter I've talked about the problems pregnancy poses, the changes it brings about, and how exercise can help you cope with them. What I've saved until last to say is what most pregnant women, at least *sometime* during their pregnancy, know well. And that is that pregnancy is an unparalleled time in a woman's life. For all its difficulties, this time of conceiving and nurturing a new life can provide a satisfaction and joy unlike any other.

For me, the primary reason to exercise is the enjoyment of doing it and the feeling of well-being it brings. By promoting health and fitness, exercise can enhance the joy of being pregnant. By helping to make the inherent physical difficulties of pregnancy less onerous, it can allow you to enjoy the experience more fully. After all, exercise helps us become more fully alive. How appropriate that it be a part of pregnancy, the time when we affirm life by creating it.

CHAPTER 7

Racing for the PaceWalker

O n May 4, 1986, I PaceWalked the *Newsday* Long Island Half Marathon.

Wait a minute. *PaceWalked* a half marathon? Half marathons are for runners, right?

Well, right. Half marathons are for runners. But they're for walkers, too. And I didn't do half bad, either. I finished the 13.1 miles in 2:45:47—that's an average pace of 12:40 minutes per mile. Although I placed 6,547th in the field, I wasn't last by any means. A total of 126 other people finished after I did, the last one a full hour and fifteen minutes behind me. And most of these people were runners—slow or tired runners, yes, but runners. In fact as I approached the finish line, PaceWalking as fast as I could go, a spectator called out, "Are you a walker?" When I nodded yes, she began applauding. But she didn't applaud the runners—only the fast walkers.

I had a great time in that race. For most of it I PaceWalked next to another walker. We pushed and paced each other all the way through the course. We worked hard, but not so hard that we couldn't keep up a conversation for the whole time we were together.

It was a typical PaceWalking experience. She was in her early forties, married, with four children. She had turned to PaceWalking several years before because of a running injury. And this was her first race ever, at any distance—what a way to start! Having observed each other keeping the same pace, we linked up shortly after the start and stayed together until there was about half a mile to go. At that point I was feeling awfully good, so I picked up the pace beyond what she was interested in doing and finished ahead of her by a couple of minutes.

During the race we talked about a lot of things: the benefits of regular exercise, the pleasures and advantages of PaceWalking (a term that was new to her at the time), other sports that we do, our respective occupations, family, children, the race itself, and the gorgeous weather. In other words, nothing earth-shattering, but in the context of the beautiful day, the race, and the sheer exhilaration of exercising, it was a typically memorable conversation. Racing can do that to you; all your senses are heightened, and the commonplace becomes special.

Finally, toward the end, we talked about how we were passing tired runners. That's another special pleasure for us racing PaceWalkers.

At the end of the race I felt the same kind of satisfaction and sweatily pleasant tiredness that I do at the end of races I've run. But there was one major difference: My feet and legs didn't hurt from thirteen miles of pounding. All PaceWalking left me with was the mild achiness that accompanies strenuous exercise. And since PaceWalking involves the upper body to a much greater extent than does running, I felt those good aches throughout my whole body. Makes you know you've done something worth doing. Makes you feel alive.

So, PaceWalkers can road race and have a good time doing it. And if you're pretty well trained and keep up a reasonably brisk pace, you can PaceWalk all the way and be virtually assured of finishing ahead of a number of runners. None of this bringing-up-the-rear business for us PaceWalkers.

Road Racing—What It Is

Road racing is just what it sounds like: racing on a road rather than on a track or a special cross-country course in a park or similar environment. The distances range from one mile, as in many local "fun runs," to miles—the Philadelphia–to–Atlantic City race, for example. But the most common distances are 5k (3.1 miles), 5 miles, 10k (6.2 miles), 10 miles, 20k (12.4 miles), half marathon (13.1 miles), and marathon (26.2 miles)—something for everyone. The races are run over measured courses on public roads. If the race is big enough, the roads are closed to vehicles and the inter-sections are monitored by police and race marshals. In smaller races, the roads are seldom closed, but the intersections are monitored and signs are posted along the way to point you in the right direction.

Most road races are for runners, or at least for people who *intend* to run the whole race. But it never fails; in every race there are people who start out running but for one reason or another end up walking part of the distance, usually rather slowly. You see those people's backs when the race starts, but later on you may PaceWalk right by them.

Increasingly, walkers are entering running road races. In fact a few running road races have entry categories for walkers by age group. The point-to-point 10k on the slopes of the Mana Kea Volcano in Hawaii, which I did in 1986, is one of those. These races are ideal for PaceWalkers who would like to have the opportunity to win an age-group medal (and, not insignificantly, have an excuse to take a trip somewhere they might not otherwise. Traveling to road races is a great way to vacation. Invariably you meet interesting people and have lots of fun). This type of race uses the honor system: As long as you don't run at any time during the race, you can qualify as a walker—using any walking gait you like.

(There are, of course, races exclusively for race walkers. PaceWalkers are welcome in them; however, to avoid disqualification, you must do the special race walking gait. But in running road races, including the run legs of triathlons, you may use any walking gait you please.)

Why Race?

There are several answers to this question. For a small proportion of road racers, those who by dint of training and natural bodily equipment are just plain fast, the objective is *to win*. That motivation is reinforced by races that provide walkers age-group medals, offering the possibility to come away with a reward for your effort beyond simple personal satisfaction. But most entrants, particularly those in the more crowded age groups, don't have a realistic chance of winning anything. They—we, I should say—race for other reasons.

Racing is *fun*. The courses are colorful, and the races are usually held in pleasant weather. There's often a happy spirit in the air that's infectious. Most of the people are worth meeting; more often than not they're attractive, reasonably healthy, and in pretty good shape. They're there, like you, not necessarily to win but simply to enjoy the race.

There you are, alone on the course. (Even when you're racing side by side with someone, you're really alone. There's always the sense of exploring the limits of one's own capabilities.) You're doing something healthy and challenging, something that not too many other people have done. And if you finish, and finish in a way that leaves you feeling good, you will really have accomplished something.

Some people race just for that *feeling of accomplishment*. It's really something very special. Particularly your first time, or when you've tackled a distance or time you thought was beyond you, the feeling of accomplishment can be overwhelming. I broke down and cried the first time I completed a 10k race. The same thing happened to me when I broke two hours in my first half marathon and when I finished my first really long triathlon. It's an intense, immensely rewarding experience. It can provide you with a level of self-esteem you've never had before.

Most road racers don't race *against* other entrants; they race *with* them. There are no opponents, really. (At least there don't have to be. Again, it all depends on *why* you're racing.) There are only the boundaries of your own body and mind and the capabilities you're attempting to explore and expand. Racing provides *the opportunity to push yourself*, to find out what you're made of.

The most challenging boundary in all sports (in anything, really) is yourself. It may feel good to pass people during a race or, as often happens toward the end, to decide to catch someone ahead of you and actually do it. But the best feeling of all is to push yourself to new accomplishments. To race a personal best time or complete a distance you previously thought was too much for you gives you a new sense of your abilities and limits.

Racing can provide a marvelous *focus for your training*. This is especially true for me. For some people it's enough to exercise for its own sake. For others, improvement in looks and fitness and the reduction in risk of disease is enough. But some people need something else to keep them going, and often that something is racing. Knowing that you're training so that you'll be able to do a particular race can be an excellent motivator.

For example, I generally start off my racing season with the Montauk (New York) Triathlon in late June. In preparation I count back thirteen weeks from the date of the race to the middle of March; that's my cue to change from my off-season maintenance program of two and a half to three hours per week to a more intensive five-hours-per-week program. While training, I usually take part in a couple of other races during the spring, but I regard these more as long workouts than as races for their own sake.

Then, after the season begins, I do several races during the summer, finishing off in the fall with a biathlon or two and perhaps a marathon. Then it's back to a reduced, winter maintenance program once again. In that way my training never has the chance to get boring or tiresome because the racing, which is so enjoyable in itself, becomes the focus of the whole endeavor.

Using racing as a focus for your training can work for you, too, regardless of the length of the races. You don't have to do marathons, for goodness sake (although I PaceWalked the 1987 New York City Marathon in 5:57:32 and had a great time). To PaceWalk a 5k or 10k road race requires a training program just as surely as do the longer races. And if you've never raced before, one of these relatively short events is the perfect way to begin. Give yourself at least three months to prepare, according to the guidelines I've suggested, then do the race. If you like it (and many people who try racing do), then you can select another or a couple more races before the season is over. Space them out comfortably—one a month, say—set up your training program around them, and before you know it you will have done an entire season of road racing without even thinking about it. Suddenly it'll be winter—time to slow down, give your body a rest, and start thinking about which races you might want to try next season. Your training has become a means to an end: racing.

PaceWalkers needn't be shy about entering road races. Even if most of the people are runners, don't worry. There are no rules requiring you to run. Most shorter races have no time limits, which means that the courses will remain open until the last person finishes. But if you can PaceWalk at a thirteen-minute-per-mile clip or better, it's unlikely you'll be the last person to finish. Almost always there are runners who are very slow or who get into trouble of one kind or another. And as the number of racing PaceWalkers continues to increase, you'll have more and more company racing at your own pace.

And remember this: Whether you're a PaceWalker, a race walker, or a runner, most race directors will be happy to have you in their race; you're paying a fee, after all. Race directors want to collect as many entrants—and as many entrance fees—as possible.

So, PaceWalkers—enter, race, and enjoy!

It must be said that racing doesn't always work out for everyone. Some people don't need it to keep up a regular workout program. Others may find that racing brings out a side of them they just don't like—those often unpleasant competitive instincts. They become tense, driven, and if they don't win—which is more likely than not—they become even more tense. Their training starts to become more stressful rather than the other way around, and the races turn into unhappy, anxiety-filled occasions rather than joyful outlets for all their hard work.

If you're one of those people, don't race. It's just not worth it. PaceWalking should be something that helps you decrease the stress and tension in your life, not make it worse. It should be fun, not torture. If racing doesn't work for you, don't give it a second thought—just don't race.

How to Start Racing

Who Organizes Races?

Races are organized by many different kinds of local organizations: running and sports clubs, churches and synagogues, hospitals, schools, universities and colleges, running and sporting goods stores, volunteer fire departments, charities, voluntary health organizations such as the American Heart Association, and private entrepreneurs. These organizers always need volunteers to help out, whether to handle registration, act as course marshals, or operate aid and water stations. If you're thinking about racing but would first like to get a feel for what it's like, try working a race as a volunteer. You'll pick up a good sense of what racing is all about, from the inside.

Where Do You Find Out About Races?

In most parts of the country, there are frequent road races in the 5k to 10k range from spring through fall. In warmer climates, there are races on almost any weekend throughout the year. You can find out about these races in a variety of places. Most running/walking shoe stores will have a stack of entry blanks for various local races. The local running and walking clubs will have them as well. For example, the New York Road Runners Club sponsors at least one race per week during most of the year and publishes annual and monthly calendars of events. National magazines such as *Runner's World, Running Times,* and *The Walking Magazine* feature race calendars and race ads. And in many parts of the country there are local magazines and newspapers that offer similar information. Last, but not least, is word of mouth. If you know a fellow walker or runner, just ask.

How Should You Choose Your First Race?

Pick a distance you think you'll be comfortable with. For your first race, a 5k or 4-mile race is probably a good choice. If you feel ambitious, try a 10k. Odds are that it won't seem nearly as long after you finish it as it did before you started.

It's a good idea to choose a race that's been run before, so that you can be reasonably assured it will be well organized and safe. Try to find a couple of people who have done it and ask them what it's like. And, all else being equal, your first race should be fairly close to home. You may be a bit nervous about doing it, so you won't want to have to drive any distance or find some obscure setting. And take a look at the course before you do the race—another good reason to pick one close to home.

As to the size of the field, you'll want one that is neither too small—because you're likely to find yourself alone on some strange road very soon after the start—or too big—being squashed or intimidated at the start is not a good way to begin your racing career. A well-run race on a good course that is not too hilly with, say, 300 to 500 entrants, will give you a great introduction to racing for its own sake. It may even encourage you to try again.

How Do You Enter?

As I've said, you can find entry blanks for races at your local running or walking shoe store. You can also get them by writing to race committees whose addresses are published in running magazines or newspapers. If you do write for a race entry blank, be sure to enclose a self-addressed, stamped no. 10 envelope. When you send the entry back, be sure to sign the release and enclose the fee; it's all too easy to forget one or more of these niggling details. And if there are race instructions or a map on the entry blank, be sure to make a copy before sending it back.

You'll almost always receive some souvenir of the race, usually a T-shirt. And it's a good idea to get entries in early, if for no other reason than late applicants may not receive a T-shirt (although most of the shorter races, 10k and under, will accept day-of-the-race applications). You can't beat a neat T-shirt—that is, until your dresser drawers are filled to overflowing with them and you can't give any more away.

Race Training for the PaceWalker

If you're racing for the fun of it, you really don't need a complicated training program. The thirteen-week Introductory Program I presented in chapter 4 is enough to prepare you for your first race, as long as it's a short one. You really shouldn't try anything over a 5k distance until you have also completed the thirteen-week Developmental Program. Then, with six good months of training behind you, you can think about doing longer races.

As a rule of thumb, you should be doing the two hours per week of the Maintenance Program if you're going to race in 5ks or 4-milers on a regular basis. For races in the 4- to 8-mile range, you should be training for about twice as many hours per week as it'll take you to finish the race. For example, if you can PaceWalk at fourteen minutes per mile, it'll take you slightly under an hour to complete a 4-mile race. So you should be on a program that provides an average of two hours of training a week.

For longer races up to half-marathon distance, you should train during the week about one and a half times as much as it takes you to finish the race. A time of 2:45 in the half marathon, for example, means about four hours of training a week. And races longer than the 13 miles of a half marathon probably need about as many hours of training per week as it takes you to finish the race. Most PaceWalkers don't race in such long events, but if you're the exception to the rule, you might turn to the Design-Your-Own Program presented in chapter 4 and set up a schedule that'll give you the average number of hours per week you'll need. I suggest that you do five workouts per week, for no longer than six hours on the average (the time it takes to do a marathon at a pace of just under fourteen minutes per mile). At the beginning of the thirteen-week period, your weekly total time should be lower than six hours; toward the end of the period it should be higher, according to the pattern of the other PaceWalking programs.

Remember, racing shouldn't be a chore. It should be fun. You may find that soon enough you'll start treating your races as little more than long workouts—although particularly enjoyable ones— part of your regular program. It's not unusual for experienced racers to do an event of 10k or less every weekend.

The Race Itself

Clothing and Equipment

Above all, dress comfortably and coolly. Many people, especially beginners, overdress for races, particularly those held on cool days. In a race you'll generally warm up even more quickly than you do while training, and in time become hotter than you are when training. On a cool day, it's a good idea to feel cool, perhaps even slightly cold, before the start. You'll heat up soon enough.

You probably won't need anything on your legs at all, unless the temperature is below 45 degrees or there's a wind-chill factor making things really uncomfortable. If you're doing a long race and are concerned about cooling down too quickly at the end, or if you're racing a point-to-point event in which the finish is some distance from the start, making it necessary for you to be bussed back to the beginning, think about carrying a light Windbreaker in a "fanny pack" that you can strap around your waist. It'll come in handy in keeping you warm after the race is over.

In hot weather you should wear as little as possible. For men, that means shorts and a racing singlet (a lightweight shirt resembling an undershirt, usually made of nylon and mesh); for women, shorts, bra, and singlet. White is the best color for keeping cool. Some people like to wear a sweat band, others a hat, and still others wear both. The point is, don't worry about what you look like; worry about keeping cool on a hot day. If there's a bright sun, you should wear sunglasses or an effective sunshield.

The last piece of equipment you'll need (besides a good pair of shoes, of course; I've gone into what to look for in shoes in some detail in chapter 3) is the stopwatch you normally use while training. You'll want to keep track of your race pace. Most races have markers every mile or two, and sometimes there are people giving "split times" at the markers (a split time is how long from the start it's taken you to arrive at that particular point)—but sometimes not. One way or another, you should be able to monitor your own per-mile pace. To do that, you have to add and subtract in your head. Admittedly, that can be hard to do in the middle of a race.

The reason for keeping track of your per-mile pace is so you'll know if you're speeding up, slowing down, or maintaining a steady pace. Most likely, it's the latter you'll be shooting for. Remember, the PaceWalking philosophy of racing is that going slowly is not a problem; going too fast, wearing yourself out, and not finishing comfortably is.

The Day of the Race

Except at the big races like the New York City Marathon, which requires you to check in beforehand, you won't have to register until the morning of the race. It's a good idea to arrive early and beat the crush that can occur at the registration tables, especially if it's a good size race. Arriving early also ensures you a parking space within reasonable proximity of the registration area. You'll be grateful for that afterwards.

You'll receive a packet that, among other things, includes your race number and souvenir T-shirt. You're not required to wear the official T-shirt during the race, but you certainly can. You'll have to pin on your race number, usually on the front of your shirt or singlet. Safety pins are almost always provided for you, but it's a good idea to bring four of your own—better safe than sorry, right?

It's important to warm up before the race. Go through your regular stretching routine, but *do not* add any new stretches for the race. Before the 1985 New York City Marathon I had some time on my hands, so I went through a series of stretches that I hadn't done in some time. By the 6-mile mark, I had severe, painful muscle spasms in my right groin. I eventually withdrew from the race at about 17 miles. The muscle just wasn't accustomed to being stretched out before a workout, and it let me know about it in no uncertain terms. It's okay to stretch, but do whatever you're accustomed to doing—no more.

Then do some PaceWalking to get the morning kinks out and break a sweat. Don't worry about diluting your stamina. If you're reasonably well trained and stay in control of your pace, you'll have more than enough endurance. Warm up by doing your arm swing as well as your leg stride. Runners only have to loosen up their legs. PaceWalkers must be concerned about their upper bodies as well.

Doing Your First Race

It's race time. You're set to go. You're suitably dressed, with your stopwatch on your wrist. You're all stretched out and warmed up, and your race number is pinned right side up in the proper place. You're probably a bit nervous, but you've trained well, and you have a good idea as to what a comfortable pace will be for you. You'll never be more ready than you are now—time to give it a shot.

As the crowd begins to form behind the starting line, stay to the rear. You'll be going slower than almost all the runners, at least at the beginning, and you don't want to get in anybody's way. You may have seen other PaceWalkers warming up. You might want to locate them before the start, find out what their race pace is, and, if it's similar to yours, ask if they might like some company on the course.

Soon the starter will announce that there are just a few minutes to go. When you hear the command to get ready, make sure your watch is set to zero. Start it going either at the gun or when you actually cross the starting line, whichever you prefer. If you start your watch as you cross the starting line, you'll know how long it's actually taken *you* to do the race distance, a time which is always less than the total elapsed time from the gun. (If there's a time limit for the race, however, it's measured from the gun, not from when you crossed the starting line.)

For the first few minutes of the race, you'll most likely be in a crowd. Keep your wits about you and PaceWalk easily. Get comfortable and relaxed, and make sure your arm swing is smooth and well coordinated with your stride. If you're racing with a partner, now's the time to make sure that each of you is comfortable with the other's pace. Then, as the field thins out, you can move into cruising mode. Concentrate on steadiness and smoothness. As you pass the mile markers, check your pace. Most likely you'll find that you're going a bit faster than your regular training pace. You feel good; the adrenaline is flowing. Just don't try to go too fast. You'll regret it later on.

Not trying to go too fast is very important in ensuring that you have fun in your races. The people who get into trouble in races, those who injure themselves or who become sick or just worn out, are usually those who go too fast at the beginning. Being able to pace yourself is extremely important, both for finishing and for staying healthy. Even if you go into a race without the proper training, maintain a rate of speed that's reasonable for the amount of training you have done, and you'll probably do just fine. Just stay within your limits.

The most important thing to do during the race—other than maintaining a steady, smooth pace, that is—is to drink the water provided at the aid stations regularly. You may not need to drink at every station, especially on a cool day, but on warm and hot days you should, at least a little. One or two cups at each station is plenty. (Some races offer an electrolyte drink as well. As most people don't become electrolyte depleted in races up to marathon length, these drinks aren't usually necessary. But it's not a bad idea to take a sip. The symptoms of electrolyte depletion are fatigue and dizziness, and there's really no way to know in advance if you're about to become depleted. So why not be on the safe side? Another way to keep your level up is to carry along a banana to munch on about halfway through. The most important electrolyte for runners is potassium, and bananas are rich in it.) And on hot days you may want to pour water over your head or splash it on your face. (Try to avoid getting your feet wet, however. Soggy socks are no fun to PaceWalk in.)

The reason for all this watering is that dehydration is the number one enemy of PaceWalkers and runners. And one of the strange features of our physiology is that by the time you feel thirsty it's already too late. You just can't catch up with your body's need for water while expending the energy to keep yourself racing at the same time. The only solution at that point is to stop, find some shade, drink and cool off, and wait for your internal body temperature to come down. Racers don't want to do that, of course, so make it a point to keep ahead of your body's needs by staying good and watered.

Once you settle into your pace, the miles will fly by, and before you know it the finish line will come into sight. If you have anything left, now's the time to turn it on. Sprint PaceWalking, which involves picking up your cadence, shortening your stride (not the other way around), and making your arm swing more compact can get you moving pretty quickly. Try to place your feet closer to that imaginary white line I talked about in chapter 3, and be sure that your breathing is comfortably synchronized with your stride—for example, breathe in for three paces, breathe out for three paces. You may find yourself bending forward a bit more as you gain momentum, but remember to do so from the hips, not the waist, so as not to constrict your breathing. I look ahead to see if there's somebody I might be able to pass and then shift into high gear. It's always fun to finish a race at top speed, feeling pretty darn good about yourself.

You cross the finish line, turn off your stopwatch, and take a look at the official time. You've done it. You are now an official road-racing PaceWalker. Whatever the distance, you've done something that you never have done before—perhaps something you never *dreamed* you'd ever do. Take a good look around you. Notice the people, the course, the day. Savor those feelings of tiredness and accomplishment. Remember those feelings. They can provide a lift for the rest of your life.

Unless you're completely exhausted—and if you've followed the recommendations in this book you most likely won't be—don't sit down. Stroll around for a bit, unwinding physically and mentally. Drink some more water and get something to eat; many races provide free food for participants. Cool down, but don't get cold. Dry off with a towel and put on something over your racing outfit. You might want to stretch a little, just to keep your tired muscles loose and relaxed. Take it easy. Feel good. Talk with family, friends, and other racers. And, if you're like most of us who race, pretty soon a funny thing will begin to happen: You'll start thinking about the next one.

CHAPTER 8

PaceWalking—
The Foundation Aerobic
SporT for PaceTraining

*T*he preceding chapters have presented many of the reasons why
PaceWalking is such a terrific aerobic sport. There's yet another
reason, one that goes beyond PaceWalking. PaceWalking can be a
wonderful entrée to other aerobic activities. It can be the foundation upon which you build a multisport exercise program. And it
can be a major component of that program as well. I call that multisport program PaceTraining.

PaceTraining is a logical extension of PaceWalking, a way to
incorporate other aerobic activities into your exercise schedule
while keeping PaceWalking at the heart of it all, your Foundation
Aerobic SporT—F.A.S.T., for short. In PaceTraining, you establish a
regular program of workouts, just as you did for PaceWalking, and
concentrate on minutes not miles, as before. But instead of doing
just one aerobic activity, you do two or more—that's the difference.
You don't increase the total time you devote to your workouts unless you want to; you simply divide that time among two or more
activities.

But why? If you're happy with PaceWalking—or running or swimming or aerobic dancing—why take on other aerobic activities?

The answer is that there's no compelling reason to do so, *if you don't want to*. Many people find PaceWalking, or any single aerobic sport, fully satisfying. They do their activity happily for years and realize significant benefits from it.

But other people, and I count myself among them, while enjoying their primary sport, like the variety that a number of different aerobic exercises brings to their workout program. If you're perfectly happy with your PaceWalking program and have no desire to change, *bravo!* By all means, stay with it. In that case, unless you're simply curious, you needn't bother to read this chapter. If, on the other hand, you feel that adding other activities to your exercise program might be fun, read on. One approach is fully as beneficial as the other. And PaceWalking can play a central role in both.

Why PaceTrain?

Because you enjoy it. That's the best reason, as far as I'm concerned. Life is too short to subject yourself to things you don't like to do—in the area of exercise, that is. But once embarked on a PaceTraining program, you may begin to realize other benefits as well.

First, *PaceTraining provides a welcome variety in your exercise*. That can be important. It may be that the most common reason people quit—or never start—aerobic exercise is that they're bored with it. Let's face it, repetitive activity isn't for everyone. Even PaceWalking, as enjoyable as so many have found it, isn't for everyone. But PaceTraining may be; at least it may be for those people who like variety in their exercise.

I like to vary my workouts. I PaceWalk and run year-round, but more in the spring and summer than other times. During the winter I usually add weight training to my workout, and from summer through fall I bicycle. It may be that I would bicycle during more of the year if our East Coast weather permitted, but I wouldn't lift weights year-round. I don't find lifting fun if I have to do too much of it. Focusing on weight training while I ease off from my other activities during the four winter months provides the right mix for me. Then when spring rolls around, I'm again ready to go outside to PaceWalk and run.

So for me, variety is important. It may be for you, as well. Variety can help keep you enthusiastic about your activities and help keep you from going stale. But it's not only psychologically that variety can be important; it can help you physically, too. That leads me to the second of the advantages of PaceTraining: *It helps provide a balanced workout program, one that exercises two or more muscle groups.*

If you come to PaceTraining from PaceWalking, of course, you're already a leg up because PaceWalking itself exercises two large muscle groups: your legs and shoulder/arms. Most aerobic activities, however, primarily exercise just one part of the body. For example, running exercises the legs. So does bicycling. Swimming, on the other hand, is primarily an upper-body sport. In fact, of the major aerobic sports, only PaceWalking and aerobic dancing will give you a relatively complete body workout.

So, if you come to PaceTraining from PaceWalking, you'll amplify the kind of thorough workout you've already been experiencing. If you come to it from running or bicycling, be prepared to exercise parts of your body that have been relatively neglected. The variety in PaceTraining offers a total-body workout that's hard to beat.

For some people, the third advantage of PaceTraining may be the most attractive of all: *The risk of injury in each of the PaceTraining activities is less than if you were doing only one activity for a comparable amount of time. In fact, it's likely that the reduced risk of injury will almost rival that of PaceWalking itself.* This is good news for runners in particular, whose sport causes more injuries than any other. Most of those injuries are overuse injuries—that is, problems caused by overusing certain parts of the body. The familiar injuries in running—shin splints, stress fractures, Achilles tendinitis, muscle strains—are all the result of the constant pounding the body takes while running. Cut down on the amount of running, and you'll reduce the number of injuries.

Cyclists are subject to some of the same overuse injuries as runners, but that's not all. They have to be on the alert for automobiles, bad road surfaces, even mechanical failures of the bikes themselves. Reduce the amount of time spent in the saddle, and you'll reduce the number of injuries.

But you *don't* reduce the quality of aerobic conditioning. That's the beauty of it. The heart doesn't differentiate among the various activities that make it work harder; all it knows is that it must work harder. If a combination of swimming, PaceWalking, and running constitutes your aerobic program, so be it. Likewise, bicycling, running, and PaceWalking. Or aerobic dancing, swimming, and PaceWalking. The combination hardly matters. What does matter is keeping your heart rate in the aerobic range.

Aerobic Activities—Ingredients for PaceTraining

Which activities should you integrate into your PaceTraining program? There are lots to choose from. Besides PaceWalking, the other major aerobic sports (so categorized because of the number of participants and general accessibility) are running, cycling, swimming, aerobic dancing, and weight training, which can be done aerobically. (Most weight training is not aerobic, however. In fact, you have to go some to make weight training aerobic. More on that a bit later on.) The minor aerobic sports include cross-country skiing, rowing, and circuit training (see following pages). The subminor aerobic sports (those done by relatively few people) are activities such as rope jumping, trampoline exercise, stair climbing, and treadmill indoor running. Any of these activities, major or minor, can provide a good aerobic workout. Choose those that appeal to you.

If you've been PaceWalking, you have a head start because not only have you already been conditioning two major muscle groups in your body, but you have a good aerobic foundation for doing any other sport. You're in good aerobic shape. But that doesn't mean that incorporating a new activity or two into your workout schedule won't cause some aches and pains. Although you may be in good aerobic condition, able to handle the cardiovascular demands of a variety of activities, your muscles will need retraining and strengthening with each new exercise. You may want to pick your aerobic activities at least partially in terms of the amount of new muscle conditioning you may have to do to handle them.

What follows is a brief description of a number of possible additions to your aerobic conditioning schedule. Since some of these activities are well known, I'll do no more here than introduce them to you and remark briefly on their benefits, aerobic and otherwise. A list of additional reading material on the most familiar of these activities is in the appendix.

Running

Running is the most popular and visible of all aerobic activities. And it hardly needs any introduction here. Suffice it to say that running, except at the slowest of paces, is a guaranteed aerobic exercise. For people of normal or near normal weight, who are otherwise healthy, and who can tolerate the pounding and jarring, it's a great sport. (Although it must be said that while there are certainly runners of all ages, it's primarily a young person's sport.) Running is cheap and convenient. It can be done outdoors or indoors (although running short indoor tracks can become mind-numbing). It provides a good workout for the lower body.

If done in moderation—at a reasonable pace for, say, no more than three to four hours per week—running offers little long-term risk of serious injury. It's when you forget about moderation and try to run too long or too fast, or neglect good and properly fitting shoes, or become too thin because of poor nutrition, that you risk injury or sickness.

Cycling

Cycling is a fine aerobic sport—some say the best of all. It's easy on the body, provides a strong workout for the legs and lower trunk, and offers a sustained aerobic workout. But it's not automatically aerobic. You have to work fairly hard at cycling to move your heart rate into the aerobic range. It's too easy to glide along at eight to ten miles per hour—not an aerobic speed for most people. Thirteen to fifteen miles per hour at a minimum is more like it, and that takes work. And it's not a particularly attractive sport to older people, especially those who are just getting into aerobic exercise, because of its demands for muscle coordination and balance.

It can be exhilarating to bicycle on a sunny day in beautiful country. This touring aspect of cycling is one of its strongest attractions. You can race as well, in events designed for bicycles only or as part of triathlons and other multisport events. And although cycling demands a bike, and so is not nearly as convenient or accessible as running or PaceWalking, it isn't as prohibitive as you might think. Just $300 to $400 will get you onto a bicycle that provides a dependable, reasonably precise ride, as well as lasts a good, long time—with proper maintenance, almost indefinitely. (Of course if you want to spend more, much more, cycling will not deny you that pleasure either. For more on bikes, see the section on equipment later in this chapter).

Yet if it can be exhilarating to get onto your bicycle, it can be anything but exhilarating to fall off. In terms of extrinsic injury (see chapter 1), bicycling is the most dangerous of all aerobic sports. And those dangers often come from circumstances outside

your control: automobiles, bad roads, other cyclists, charging animals, and slick surfaces, for example.

One way around that, and also the problem of inclement weather, is to bicycle indoors. Riding stationary bikes has become a staple aerobic activity. The bicycles take two forms: exercise bikes and regular road bikes mounted on various devices that allow them to be used indoors. The more common of those, of course, is the exercise bike, which you can adjust to provide resistance, assuring you an aerobic workout.

The problem with biking indoors is boredom. Many people combat boredom by working out in front of the TV. In fact, working out while watching the evening news is becoming a popular activity (especially when a drink and a meal in the not-too-distant future is your reward). Just be sure not to become so involved with the tube that you forget to pump those pedals.

Other people deal with boredom in more imaginative ways. As an example, I can't resist telling this story about my father. Now seventy-eight years old, Dad was a fine swimmer and runner as a young adult. Then, as happens to so many of us, he became busy with his career and family and stopped exercising regularly. It wasn't until his early seventies that he decided it was time to become physically active again. So he bought an indoor exercise bike.

Now his problem was boredom—especially because soon Dad was chalking up as much as five miles on the bike's odometer each day. He came up with a novel solution: He began making imaginary trips along the country roads around his home that he knew so well. Then, after thoroughly exploring the local countryside, he pulled out a road atlas and began cycling west—all this, mind you, in the familiar territory of his own mind and his own living room. By now he's cycled all the way to the West Coast and back, twice.

But the best is yet to come. On his way back from his first "trip" to the Coast, Dad scheduled a stop in Flagstaff, Arizona. He happened to mention his imaginary journey to a friend who, it turns out, knew Flagstaff's mayor. Dad's friend spoke to the mayor, who in turn notified the local newspaper. And soon Dad received a phone call from a reporter at the newspaper who interviewed him for forty-five minutes. On the day Dad "arrived" in Flagstaff, an article and photo were published in the newspaper announcing his presence in town and detailing the rest of his trip. He arrived home from that journey without incident, and then took off on his second transcontinental voyage, to the west coast of Canada.

Swimming

There may be no aerobic activity that's so easy on the body as swimming. Gliding along, with none of the pounding and jarring of other aerobic sports (a blessing *and* a disadvantage—more on that in a minute), cushioned and supported on all sides by water, a swimmer can enjoy one of the most effective and safe workouts of all (assuming you know how to swim, that is—if not, it's not so safe). The injury rate is low. People who swim swear by it.

As I said earlier, swimming is mainly an upper-body sport, but your lower body can get some work if, say, you do breast stroke or use fins. But you have to work pretty hard to sustain an aerobic effect. And you don't get the benefits of working against gravity—increased bone mass and strength. That's why swimming may be an especially good exercise to do in combination with others. Swimming does nothing to help prevent osteoporosis in women, for example, in contrast to weight-bearing activities like running, cycling, and PaceWalking. So, when done along with activities that utilize gravity, swimming can provide a very fine workout.

The main problem with swimming is its inconvenience. You need a pool, and once you find one, you must adhere to its workout schedule. Limited lap time often produces jam ups and multiple flailing arms per lane. In such cases, the joy of swimming can quickly escape any but the most devoted.

I prefer open-water swimming. It has its own problems, of course. Limited availability (not much open water in Kansas or New Mexico, for example), high or choppy waves, wind, cold water, and limited visibility are just a few of them. And many people don't like being in the open water when they don't know what may be swimming beneath them. But there are no pool schedules to adhere to, no lanes to share, usually no fees to pay—and the exhilaration of swimming in the great outdoors.

Aerobic Dancing

For women, aerobic dance is the most popular organized sporting activity in the country—more than all high school P.E. classes put together. It can be done at home, of course, but most people prefer doing it in groups; that means fees and the inconvenience of finding a health club and adhering to schedules. It's also a preferred way of meeting people of the opposite sex, especially since more and more men are doing aerobic dance.

Aerobic dance conditions the entire body, and the injury rate is surprisingly low, especially with low-impact aerobics. (A common way of injuring yourself is trying to do what the instructor does. Aerobic instructors have had all sorts of training that you most likely haven't had. When an instructor demonstrates a step, she usually does so with a flexibility and élan you may not be able to muster. It's important to respect your own limits in aerobic dance classes. The sessions are *not* supposed to be competitions.) And when you aerobic dance in a group, it can be the least boring of any aerobic activity. Many people are attracted to it for that reason alone.

Weight Training

Weight training can be very good exercise, but for the most part it's not aerobic exercise. Remember, for an activity to offer aerobic benefits it must push your heart rate into the aerobic range for at least twenty minutes. That's twenty minutes *straight,* not twenty minutes altogether. So repetitive, endurance activities like PaceWalking, running, swimming, and cycling are perfect for aerobic benefits. They readily push your heart rate into the aerobic range and, because there are no pauses in the activity, they keep it there. Other sports such as tennis, baseball, volleyball, bowling, golf, and even basketball may be lots of fun and good for you in their way, but they don't offer consistent aerobic benefits. There's too much standing around as compared to moving around.

Weight training most often falls into this latter category. Certainly working hard on a Nautilus machine, for example, doing your two or three sets of twelve reps, will drive your heart rate into the aerobic range. But then what do most people do afterwards? Take a breather for a minute or two before moving on to the next apparatus. And that minute or two can stretch to a few minutes or more in a busy health club where vacant weight machines are at a premium. So that hard-won aerobic heart rate quickly slows down to normal. Then it's on to the next machine, build up the heart rate, cool down between stations—and so it goes.

If you'd like to make *aerobic* weight training part of your PaceTraining regimen, you must make a concerted effort to move from one station to another quickly enough so that your heart rate does not have a chance to slow down. Remember, at least twenty minutes of *sustained* aerobic workouts at least three times a week is the minimum recommended by the American College of Sports Medicine.

That said, weight training can be very good exercise, whether aerobic or not. Going through a complete course of weight-training equipment exercises the entire body, stretching it as well as building muscle. Working out with free weights builds muscle dramatically, of course. But be very careful. Although once you get the knack of it you can use weight-training machines by yourself with relatively little risk of injury, you should never lift free weights without a partner, and never without some instruction beforehand. Better yet is to lift in a gym along with other lifters who know what they're doing.

Weight training can be aerobic exercise, but often isn't. It's also relatively inconvenient for most people (unless you're in the tiny minority that has a home gym), comparatively expensive because of club fees or the cost of equipment, and, in the case of free weights, dangerous if not done correctly. It must be done with particular care, but in that case weight training can be a fine exercise—and an aerobic one.

Cross-Country Skiing

I've called cross-country skiing—or ski touring, as it's often termed—and rowing and circuit training minor aerobic sports because relatively few people do them regularly. But there's nothing minor about their effectiveness as aerobic exercise. In fact, cross-country skiing may be the best sport of all. It exercises the entire body, as anyone trying it for the first time will tiredly admit by the end of the day. Most people find it relatively easy to learn. It's done against gravity, so that your bones tend to grow in density and strength, but it's a smooth, rhythmic sport like cycling, and has none of the pounding that's associated with running. Like running, you don't have to push too hard to realize aerobic benefits. And it's a particularly refreshing and invigorating sport.

Unfortunately, despite the boom in cross-country skiing (as the expense of downhill skiing continues to rise and lift lines become longer), the sport obviously isn't accessible to most people on a regular basis. First and foremost it requires snow, cold weather, and a suitable place to do it. It also requires equipment, which, while not as costly as downhill gear, still involves a healthy investment. And it's a time-consuming activity—no half-hour jaunts to the slopes and back. (There are several indoor cross-country ski machines that give you a good workout without having to leave home, if you can deal with the problem of boredom.)

Rowing

Rowing has much in common with cross-country skiing, in both its advantages and its problems. It's a tough, energetic activity, with strong aerobic benefits. The injury risk is relatively low. And it provides a good workout for the upper as well as the lower body.

But it's neither cheap, convenient, nor easy to learn. It can be hard to find suitable stretches of water, the time commitment is a heavy one, and, depending on where you live, the seasons can severely restrict your workout; it's hard to row on a frozen lake. As with cross-country skiing, there are indoor rowing machines that provide an excellent workout.

Circuit Training

Circuit training is an aerobic routine found in some health clubs. A recorded voice guides you through a circuit of stations, each one of which requires you to do a certain exercise. For example, you may alternate working out on a weight machine with bursts of aerobic exercise on a stationary bike or a trampoline. You must do the exercises in the order prescribed and in the time allotted. In other words, no malingering. Later, if you want, you can go back through the circuit again—and again and again. Exercising in the mechanical age.

I don't do circuit training, but I think it can provide a good workout. But to do it you have to join a club, and not just any club—a club that offers circuit training. Those can be relatively hard to find. No matter how beneficial, circuit training is not for everyone.

Other Aerobic Activities

Jumping rope can provide a terrific aerobic workout—indeed, an exhausting one. It also can be one of the most enjoyable of the solitary aerobic activities, since people often jump rope to music. It can seem more like dancing than working out.

Like running, jumping rope can cause a great deal of pounding to ankles, knees, and back. But unlike running, it conditions the upper and lower body. It's an accessible, convenient way of working out and, in contrast to most of these activities, can be done equally well both indoors and out.

The Principles of PaceTraining

After you've picked an activity—or activities—to add to your PaceWalking, the next step is to begin to PaceTrain. The principles are similar to those of PaceWalking.

First establish your goals. Figure out why you want to PaceTrain and what it is that you want to accomplish. For most people, among the primary goals of PaceTraining are benefiting your health, improving your fitness, enhancing your appearance, and having fun. Racing may be a goal as well, but it doesn't have to be.

Second, establish a regular, planned, ongoing exercise program.

Third, the bottom line for effectiveness in any PaceTraining program is your heart rate and how long that heart rate is maintained. Any activity that raises your heart rate into the aerobic range and keeps it there is just as good aerobically as any other activity. And workouts are measured in minutes, not miles.

Fourth, the proper pace of PaceTraining is one that allows you to meet your goals. There are no universal rules here. Each PaceTrainer's program may be different (more on that in a minute). But consistency and regularity, as discussed in chapter 2, are essential.

Finally, it's important to understand that while PaceTraining, like PaceWalking, is designed to be fun, it's neither magic nor painless. There are no instant one-minute, or five-minute, or twelve-minute ways to become healthy and fit through exercise. To realize the benefits of aerobic exercise, you need to devote both time and effort. PaceTraining, like PaceWalking, requires commitment.

"Pace" in PaceTraining

The key to succcessful aerobic exercising is pace. And in PaceTraining, as in PaceWalking, pace can mean a number of things.

The most obvious, of course, is your heart's pace as it does its aerobic work. Another is the pace at which you do your workouts. In PaceTraining, as in PaceWalking, that pace need only be fast enough to push your heart rate into the aerobic range. It doesn't matter how fast you run or bike or swim, as long as your heart's beating above 70 percent of its maximum rate (and, for safety's sake, not over 85 percent of its maximum).

This sense of pace spills over into triathlon, the racing event for PaceTrainers. Pacing during a triathlon is critical to success, and how you pace depends on what your goals are. When I race, my goal is to finish. It's nice to better my previous best time, of course, but primarily I want to finish, happily and healthfully. I want to enjoy the race, not agonize through it. So I decide ahead of time how fast I think I'll be able to go and what pace I must maintain to get there. And then I stick to it.

That's often easier said than done. Sometimes you feel so good at the beginning of a race that you're tempted to go faster than you're capable of going. Your adrenaline is up, the possibilities seem infinite, why not push it? Well, you pay for such intemperance later on when you run into the wall, so to speak. So the good endurance racer knows what pace works best and sticks to it.

The same is true of your workouts. Don't try to push too hard too soon; you'll regret it later. Often, doing too much too soon results in injury—our bodies just aren't built to rush into things. And injuries, besides being painful or debilitating in themselves, set your exercise program back. A hasty, overdone beginning, then an injury, and you may find yourself worse off than when you began. Take it easy.

Pace also refers to setting a year-round exercise schedule that works for you. For example, you may want to vary your pace according to the season. During triathlon season, which lasts from late spring through early fall in the New York area, where I live, I PaceWalk, run, bike, and swim, averaging some five to six hours a week of training. In the middle of fall, after the racing season is over, I cut back to two and a half to three hours per week, running or PaceWalking once or twice, swimming regularly, bicycling occasionally (some indoors), and usually adding some weight training. Come spring, I drop the weights and start anew to prepare for my first triathlon. That seems to give me the variety I need. I come fresh to each change of season, maintaining my conditioning base during the winter months so that I can hit it hard during the summer.

Pace in PaceTraining also refers to the fact that you set your own pace for yourself. No one can do it for you, really. Guides such as this book can help, especially when you're just starting out, but when it comes down to it, you're the only one who knows what you need and what you want. That's why setting reasonable goals is so important.

In PaceTraining, *you* control the training; you don't let it control you. For most of us, exercise training, no matter what it is, should not become the be-all and end-all of our lives. No workout regimen, no matter how rigorous, should disrupt your work or break up your home. That kind of disproportionate dedication is neither healthy nor necessary to become fit. In PaceTraining, if you establish reasonable goals, design your training program accordingly, and stick to it regularly and consistently, you'll almost invariably meet those goals—and, at the same time, the whole of your life will remain in balance.

Setting Goals

There are two steps to the process. The first is to figure out just why you're interested in PaceTraining in the first place. The second is to set goals that are achievable.

I decided to start exercising because I wanted to practice what I preached. As a specialist in preventive medicine, I wanted to live my philosophies to the fullest extent possible. Still, it took real dissatisfaction with my own level of fitness to make me finally turn intent into action.

My reasons had nothing to do with running as far or as fast as a Bill Rodgers or bicycling with the speed and endurance of a Greg LeMond. I just wanted to *feel* better and do what I advised other people to do. And in PaceWalking and PaceTraining, I found activities perfect for me. Immediately, though, it was clear to me that I'd never be a champion in any of the PaceTraining events. I determined that I would PaceTrain for health and fitness primarily and try to complete and enjoy races as well.

I'm happy to say that so far I've fulfilled those goals, and more. I've had more fun with PaceTraining than I ever thought possible. I'm in better condition than I ever thought possible. And I feel better about myself than I ever thought possible—certainly better than I did before I began exercising.

That's my experience; you can do the same. You can achieve as much as I have, or more, or less—it really doesn't matter. What does matter is that you achieve goals that are reasonable for you. So approach your PaceTraining with an eye toward what you want to get out of it. And then tailor your schedule accordingly.

PaceTraining and Cross-Training

This is probably the best place to interject a note about cross-training, the natural ancestor of PaceTraining. Athletes have cross-trained for years. Cross-training is nothing more than training in two or more sports at the same time, but usually for purposes different from those I've suggested for PaceTraining. For the most part, people have cross-trained for one of three reasons: (1) to deal with injury (mainly for runners); (2) to improve single sport performance; (3) to train for triathlon racing. In other words, people cross-train for reasons beyond the benefits of the training itself, as a means to an end. However, as far as I'm concerned there need be no reason to PaceTrain beyond your enjoyment in the doing. For PaceTrainers, the training itself can be its own end.

That's not to say, however, that PaceTrainers won't enjoy the same benefits as those who cross-train. And those benefits are many and varied. Exercise physiologists Tom LaFontane and Liz Bulman's 1986 article in *Triathlon* magazine was one of the first to look at cross-training for its own sake. They came up with the following eleven advantages to cross-training. I offer them here because they so succinctly describe many of the benefits of PaceTraining as well, some of which I've already suggested, some of which may be a surprise.

1. Cross-training reduces the risk of overuse injury in any of the sports comprising the training program.

2. It improves cardiovascular performance without putting undue strain on any one major muscle group.
3. It provides for total aerobic fitness of both upper and lower body.
4. Since you don't use the same muscle groups each day, it allows for greater daily intensity of training.
5. Since swimming promotes an increase in lung capacity, running and cycling performance may be benefited. (Not to mention PaceWalking.)
6. It promotes muscle balance.
7. Since cycling strengthens the quadriceps muscles in the thigh, uphill running may be benefited by doing it.
8. Cross-training may promote improved physiological efficiency in the utilization of oxygen—one of the prime benefits of any aerobic exercise.
9. Swim training increases the strength and endurance of your respiratory system.
10. Cross-training provides variety to your regimen and helps avoid boredom.
11. Cross-training helps promote recovery from injuries.

That's a pretty impressive list.

PaceWalking to PaceTraining— A Natural Progression

The key to PaceTraining is being in aerobic shape. There's more to it than that, of course. Proper technique in the various activities is important, as is the right combination of activities for you. You'll also exercise new muscles, experience some new aches and pains. But if you're in good aerobic shape to begin with, you'll have a foundation that will stand you in good stead throughout your PaceTraining.

Once PaceWalking has put you in aerobic shape, you can maintain that level of fitness by continuing to do aerobic sports—any of them in any combination. PaceWalking enables you to begin other aerobic activities without having to learn them and get in shape at the same time. And PaceWalking can remain with you as an integral part of your PaceTraining program, either continuously or periodically. It's really the ideal way to start exercising, and the ideal activity to keep as the heart of your aerobic workout program.

How to PaceTrain

With PaceWalking, it was easy: Just get out and walk. That's the special appeal of PaceWalking—it's so easy to do. Add a bit of discipline, a jot of commitment, a modicum of scheduling, some modest attention to technique, and you're off and running—off and *walking,* that is.

PaceTraining is not quite so simple. Now you must deal with two or more activities, not just one. When you start talking about running, bicycling, swimming, or any of the other possible PaceTraining ingredients, you're getting into things that aren't quite so easy as walking. Anyone can pretty much get out and run, I suppose, but after that, things get a bit more difficult. Most people know how to ride—or at least not to fall off—a bicycle, and many people know how to swim—how to stay afloat, that is. But there's a big difference between riding around the block and riding for twenty minutes or more at an aerobic pace. And there's also a big difference between keeping your head above water and doing twenty minutes of aerobically efficient laps.

With PaceTraining we get into technique, equipment, and, in the case of swimming, a pool or a warm and calm enough body of water. And when you move toward aerobic dancing, weight training, and cross-country skiing, the difficulties begin to multiply. An instructor, a place to do it, equipment, training, proper form, the risk of injury—now we're getting into complicated territory.

This book is not the place to go into all that, for obvious reasons. I'll do no more here than comment briefly on all these considerations. If you're interested in hearing more, there's a list of useful reading matter on the major PaceTraining sports in the appendix. But if you're new to any of these activities, the best thing is to get some good, live instruction. Nothing can take the place of that.

Consistency and Regularity

To realize lasting aerobic benefits, PaceTraining *must* be done consistently; that is, during workout sessions that are reasonably close to the same length—and regularly—every other day or so. Your workouts should *not* be bunched together at the end of the week. Spread them out. And be concerned with minutes, not miles. If you ignore how long you exercise in favor of how far, you may not realize any aerobic benefits at all. To swim a mile at a shot is admirable, but unless that mile includes at least twenty minutes in which your heart rate is in the aerobic range, you're missing out. Time is what is important in aerobic exercise, not distance.

The Importance of Progressing Gradually

As important as progressing gradually may be for the PaceWalker, it's even more important for the PaceTrainer. Once you begin to throw in a number of activities, to mix and match, so to speak, it's easy to lose track of what you're doing and why you're doing it. It's also easy to overdo.

Remember why you're exercising. Remember that new activities make different demands on the body from those you're used to. Don't overdo. If anything, cut down until your body can adjust to the new activity. Learn to recognize when you need a break and when you need to push yourself. And above all, remember that you're exercising for *yourself,* not to satisfy some arbitrary criteria as to how fit you should be or how hard you should work out. Progressing gradually puts *you* in control of your activities. (In my book, *Triathloning for Ordinary Mortals,* see appendix 2, I offer training schedules, similar in design to those in chapter 4, to help you do just that.)

Elements of Technique

There's really no room to go into the intricacies of technique here. If you're interested, there are plenty of good books and articles available—I've listed some favorites in appendix 2. But nothing beats real, live instruction. If in doubt, *take a lesson*.

Good technique is important, whether the activity is relatively simple—running, for example—or complicated—swimming, for instance. You don't have to have great technique, but you do need to know what you're doing. For example, if your swim stroke is at the level of the "Coney Island crawl" (which is, for the benefit of non–New Yorkers, swimming with your head always out of the water and moving from side to side with each stroke, always accompanied by a great deal of splashing), you may get a good aerobic workout, but you'll exhaust yourself in the process. And in rough water, or during long races, such exhaustion can be dangerous. (Although in the 1985 Cape Cod Endurance triathlon, I swam much of the 2.4-mile course in the company of a young man who did the Coney Island crawl for the whole of the ninety-six minutes it took both of us to finish. Not only was he in extraordinary shape, as you might expect, but he had only one leg to boot.)

Good technique will make whatever sport you're doing more comfortable and more fun. It'll give you a feeling of being in control, which is important. And it can help avoid ordinary aches and pains and extraordinary injuries. For example, in cycling, proper gear selection is vitally important. You don't want to get caught pedaling up a hill using a gear that's too high. Good riders use a technique called "spinning," in which they pedal at high rpm in a relatively low gear. The preferred cadence, as it's called, for the training cyclist is 80 to 100 rpm. This cadence improves efficiency, increases endurance (thus raising average speed during your workout), reduces thigh burn, and saves wear and tear on your knees.

It's the knees, as you might expect, that suffer the most injuries in cycling. The most common knee injury is "biker's knee," an inflammation of the underside of the kneecap. It's most often caused by pedaling too slowly, with too much effort on each stroke, in a gear that's too high. Spinning can help prevent the injury.

So you don't have to become a technique fanatic, but you might spend some time on it. Good technique will make all your PaceTraining activities more enjoyable and more productive.

Equipment

Finally, there's equipment. With PaceWalking, all you really need are good shoes and a stopwatch. In PaceTraining, a good pair of shoes is still the most important piece of equipment for many of the sports, but there's a lot more to consider. (For more information than I present here, refer to the books listed in appendix 2.)

Running and PaceWalking Shoes

First, your shoes must fit well and be comfortable. Those are by far the most important qualities to look for, no matter what the activity. If your shoes don't feel good, they'll be of little use to you despite all their advertised features. Before you buy shoes, test them inside the store. If the store permits it, PaceWalk or run outside. Spend as long as you can using them because they certainly won't feel any better later on. Usually a shoe that doesn't fit well in the store isn't going to loosen or tighten in time to make a difference. Most often, what you feel is what you get.

Second, your shoes should be properly designed for the activity for which you're going to use them. Although distinctions may blur a bit from time to time (and economics is certainly a factor here), it's not a good idea to use your aerobic shoes for running or your cycling shoes for PaceWalking. And you really shouldn't run in your PaceWalking shoes or vice versa. Each of them has features appropriate to the activity at hand.

For example, a good running shoe should provide cushioning and support for the heel and a modest degree of flexibility in the forefoot. The cushioning should be soft enough to be comfortable, but not so soft that it flattens out under pressure, thereby doing you little good. And good running shoes are built with resistive material along the inside edge, to help keep you from overly pronating (that is, rolling your ankles to the inside) as you run.

PaceWalking shoes, on the other hand, don't need nearly as much heel cushioning as do running shoes. The reason is obvious: You don't come down on your heel as hard in walking as you do in running. But the shoes need more flexibility in the forefoot than do running shoes because PaceWalkers' feet bend more sharply at the end of the stride than runners' feet do.

Running shoes have been around for quite some time, of course. Walking shoes are a more recent development. Any good athletic shoe store should have both.

Aerobic Dance Shoes

Aerobic dance shoes need cushioning under the ball of the foot, which is where you land in most aerobic dance routines. Most aerobic dance shoes do provide some cushioning in this area, but beware of cushioning that's too soft. If the shoes feel soft when you first step into them, most likely they'll be too soft to protect your feet when you start to pound around in aerobics dance class. Look for the firmest pair you can find that is still comfortable.

Test the shoe in the store by doing some moves from your aerobics class. Don't just walk in them; get up on your toes and bounce around. Point your toe to make sure the heel counter doesn't cut into the back of your foot. And be sure it's aerobic *dance* shoes that you're trying on, not just aerobic shoes. There are some general aerobic shoes on the market that are advertised to be good for all aerobic sports. Don't believe it. With all the different requirements of the various aerobic activities, it's impossible for one shoe to work for all.

If you become a PaceTrainer, you may end up with a closetful of shoes, each of which has only one use.

Bicycle Shoes

Shoes are not the most important equipment in cycling, of course, but they're worth being careful about. For example, you should not use running shoes for cycling. They're not rigid enough, and as you become a proficient rider, you'll find that running shoes are so flexible that they allow your heel to fall below the level of the pedal during your downstroke, and you'll lose a significant portion of your power. Furthermore, running shoes tend to have wide soles, which can be hard to get into pedal toe-clips and even harder to get out of, especially in an emergency.

There are three types of cycling shoes: (1) touring shoes, (2) racing shoes with cleats that grab onto a ridge across the back of the pedal, and (3) a new variety that does away with the conventional pedal altogether and attaches directly to the pedal arm by a spring-loaded device.

Each of these has its advantages; the right one for you all depends on what kind of riding you plan to do. The new spring-loaded pedal/cleat combination is catching on very fast among cyclists, especially after it was used by the winners of the 1985 and 1986 Tours de France races. You snap in and twist out. This new shoe allows you to attach firmly to the pedal bar, but release quickly in the case of an emergency—something you can't do if you're strapped into a toe-clip or connected to the pedal by the cleats on the bottom of the shoe. And there's no toe-clip to put pressure on your toes. As you might imagine, however, the new shoes and pedals are more expensive than other models.

Bicycles

Although the cost of bikes can quickly enter the stratosphere, you can buy a perfectly good bike for no more than $300 to $450.

You can buy a bettter one for $450 to $600. But if you can't afford to spend even the lower figure right now, wait. Unless it's a quality bike that happens to be on sale, which sometimes happens with discontinued models, a cheaper bike won't be worth buying. The most important requirements for a worthwhile bike are a "chrome-moly" steel alloy frame and alloy wheels. Anything else is just too heavy and will make for uncomfortable, unresponsive biking. The cheaper bikes have all-steel frames, which may not feel heavy at first, but will seem to put on weight very quickly on a steep hill or long jaunt. Besides, if you become at all interested in biking, you'll soon be in the market for a better bike anyway.

As for the more expensive bikes with super-steel, aluminum, or carbon-fiber frames, I'd suggest that you wait. See if you really like cycling first. Besides, you'll have to learn a lot about riding before you'll be able to appreciate the features of the more expensive frames and be able to select the type that's best for you. One feature worth looking for in your first bike, however, is the new "indexed" shift mechanism, which makes shifting much easier and more precise. (There are inexpensive versions that appear even on low-end bikes.) And most important of all—fully as important as the bike itself—is a hard-shell helmet. *You should wear a helmet at all times.* A good one will cost you from $25 to $50. Think of your head as an egg and your brain as the yoke. Falling off your bike onto your head is much like dropping an egg onto the pavement. Wear a helmet.

Weight-Training Machines

Free weights are relatively inexpensive, but, although it can be done, lifting free weights generally doesn't afford you an aerobic workout. Besides, working with free weights requires a partner. If you want to achieve an aerobic workout with weights, and you want to be able to exercise by yourself, you're pretty much stuck with weight-training machines.

You're not really "stuck," of course, for weight-training machines can provide a very good workout. But using them leads you firmly into the world of inconvenience and expense. It's hard to find affordable weight-training machines that are good for you, safe, and durable. Machines costing less than $1,000 may not last if you use them regularly over a prolonged period of time. That includes those made of plain steel or that provide resistance with springs, or hydraulic mechanisms.

If you're going to spend that kind of money, you better be convinced that you're going to use the machine for a while. Join a health club that's known to have a good weight-training program and qualified instructors, at least for a three-month trial membership. See if you like it. If you do, *then* you might think about buying yourself a machine.

Where to Buy Equipment

Unless you know a lot about what you're going to buy, or have the means to find out, you're pretty much dependent on the advice of salespeople. That can be a mixed blessing. Sometimes you'll find knowledgeable people who are interested in helping you as well as in making a sale, sometimes not. And when you're a neophyte, it can be hard to tell one category from the other.

There's no foolproof method for finding accurate and helpful advice, of course, but there is one useful rule of thumb: In general you're better off buying equipment in stores that specialize in selling that equipment. For example, you'll be best off in what is called a pro shop—one staffed by riders and patronized by people who wear helmets and black bike shoes. The most expensive bike in the store will sell for at least twice what you're planning to spend. If so, you know that you're in a store where the staff knows what it's doing. You're more likely to find salespeople who know and actually use the equipment they sell than if you buy at a department or discount store. You're also more likely to find people who can advise from personal experience and interpret for you the comments of other exercisers.

The drawback to shopping at the specialty stores is, of course, price. They tend to be more expensive than the discount stores.

Some people browse at the specialty stores and then, when they've found out what they want to know, buy at the discount stores or through mail order. That doesn't make the specialty store people very happy, but they're used to it by now. I make no moral judgments here. You're on your own with this one. But do remember, by and large the specialty stores will stand behind what they sell.

Clothing

A final word, on clothing. It's possible to spend lots and lots of money on aerobic clothing. But it's not necessary. Most people can outfit themselves from their closet and, if not, there are lots of great, modern fabrics, bright colors, and flattering styles available for under $50. After all, how much clothing do you need for most of these activities? Not much. When you're just starting out, it's a good idea to spend your money on necessary equipment first, then buy clothes later. A good pair of shoes or the right bike is worth a roomful of attractive shorts and tanktops. Then, when you're certain that you're going to stick with the sport, go out and buy that spiffy outfit you've been eyeing.

A Last Word

So, that's a quick course in preparing to PaceTrain. All that remains is to choose the sport or sports you want and do them regularly. You might PaceWalk two days a week, swim once, and cycle twice. Or vice versa. Or any combination thereof. You can mix and match sports as you please, as long as you get in your aerobic time. You can build your own program based on Maintenance or Maintenance Plus in chapter 4. Alternatively, you can refer to the various sport-specific programs in the triathlon training books listed in appendix 2. PaceTraining will not necessarily add time to your program. It simply adds variety, which may or may not be just what the doctor ordered—this doctor, that is. If the idea appeals to you, why not give it a try?

CHAPTER 9

Exercise and Health

*E*xercise is in the news. We read about it in newspaper and magazine articles. We watch TV programs about it. Videotapes exhort us to do more and more of it. Books, like this one, present thorough exercise programs. All of this must mean that exercise is good for us, right? So good, in fact, that some people talk about it as though it were a cure for anything that's wrong with our bodies.

But then every once in a while we hear something just the opposite. For example, a 1986 issue of *U.S. News & World Report* featured the headline, "Easy Does It! The New Rules of Exercise: Life in the slow lane can be good for your health." And in 1984, Cornell Medical School cardiologist Henry Solomon wrote a book called *The Exercise Myth*. In it he challenged the notion that exercise is good for health. Solomon came down especially hard on running, claiming that it's actually harmful to health. (He did, though, begrudgingly endorse walking for those who feel that they must exercise.)

So what's a body to think? Is exercise a panacea or is it useless or maybe even harmful? Well, let's put the confusion to rest once and for all: While no panacea, exercise done in a healthy manner is very good for our health. It helps us feel better, *right now*. It helps us reduce the risk of developing several major diseases and unhealthy conditions. It's useful in the treatment and management of a number of diseases and conditions. Moreover, exercise can actually help protect us from developing these problems in the first place. For example, in 1987, having reviewed all of the statistics concerning the relationship of aerobic exercise and heart disease published in English, the United States Public Health Service concluded that *lack* of exercise carries with it a definite risk of heart disease—as great as that of high blood pressure, high cholesterol levels in the blood, and cigarette smoking. They also concluded that because more people are sedentary than suffer from the other risk factors, for the population as a whole *there's no better preventive measure against heart disease than exercising*. Exercise is simply one of the most effective, and most enjoyable, strategies available to increase the quality of our lives.

It's not just any old exercise I'm talking about but, rather, aerobic exercise. If you can improve your heart's ability to pump blood, and therefore your body's ability to utilize what that blood provides—life-giving oxygen—you'll be healthier as a result. That's not to say that nonaerobic exercise is bad for you. It's certainly better than nothing. Nonaerobic exercise may limber you up, strengthen your muscles, help you feel better about yourself, and help you lose weight, but it does little to protect you directly from problems like heart disease and high blood pressure. So from now on when I say "exercise," I mean aerobic exercise.

Exercise, Health, and Balance

The key to healthful exercising is to be found in one word: *balance*. If you don't exercise enough, you won't realize the benefits. But if you exercise too much, or do a type of exercise that's not right for you, you may actually be harmed by it. The process is an expression of one of the miracles of the human body—homeostasis.

Homeostasis is a state of balance in our bodies. The word also describes a very complex process, a set of mechanisms that the body uses to achieve, maintain, and reacquire balance when things go a bit haywire. Think about it. Not eating enough food is unhealthy. Eating too much food is also unhealthy. If you don't get enough air to breathe, that's unhealthy; breathing too deeply or too quickly—that is, hyperventilating—also is unhealthy. Not having enough iron in your blood is bad for you, a condition called anemia. But having too much iron in your blood isn't good either, because it can lead to a serious disease called hemochromatosis. Not drinking enough water is bad; drinking too much is also bad. And so on and so on.

Likewise, if exercise is to be beneficial, if it is to promote health and contribute to your feeling of well-being, it must be balanced. And it must be balanced in three areas. The *kind* of exercise you do must be appropriate, and the *amount* and *intensity* must be appropriate as well. If you fall short in any category, you might as well not exercise at all. Balance is that important.

Balanced Running

As an example of balance, let's take a look at running, the most publicized of aerobic sports and the anti-exerciser's favorite whipping boy. Running will kill your knees and ruin your back, they say. Fred A. Stutman, M.D., actually claims that running will *kill* you. The first chapter of his book *Walk, Don't Die* is entitled, "Dead Joggers Tell No Tales." Well . . . at least Dr. Stutman likes walking. But, of course, running does none of these things. The truth is that, done moderately, running presents little hazard at all.

It's said that running causes arthritis and other muscle and joint problems. Yet in 1986, two studies that looked for an association between running and osteo- (that is, degenerative) arthritis, published in the *Journal of the American Medical Association*, found nothing of the sort. Each compared a group of longtime runners with a group of nonrunners comparable in age, sex, and state of health. It turned out that there was no difference between the two groups in the rate of occurrence of osteoarthritis. In fact, there were no differences between the two groups in the frequency of pain and swelling of hips, knees, ankles, feet, and other mus-culoskeletal complaints. That's not to say that no one will *ever* get osteoarthritis from running. But the studies demonstrated that peo-ple who have not suffered joint injuries can run for many years and suffer no increased risk of ill effects on their musculoskeletal sys-tems over the nonrunning population.

However, as we've seen, there can be too much of a good thing. Dr. Kenneth Cooper, who first came up with the term aero-bics, says that people who work out more than the equivalent of running fifteen to twenty miles per week—that is, more than about three hours a week—receive no increased health benefits for their trouble. Whether they know it or not, they're working out for rea-sons other than health. They're working out for improved fitness, but even fitness improvement has its limits. Studies by Dr. David Costill have found that you can increase your level of fitness by exercising up to the equivalent of running seventy-five miles per week—about ten hours a week for a moderately fast runner. Be-yond that point, your effort offers little improvement in fitness. (Fit-ness and health are not the same thing; I'll review the difference again in a moment.)

Still, people often think that the more they do, the better off they are. In fact, they don't realize that they may *not* be better off in terms of health and fitness, but if they overdo their running work-outs, for example, they're also more likely to suffer common run-ning injuries like shin splints and blisters.

Such injuries are not necessary. For example, 1987 marked my seventh year of regular running, and I've never had an overuse injury. I also rarely run more than twenty miles a week. In com-bination with my other activities, that distance gives me more than enough exercise to stay healthy and reasonably fit and doesn't break me down in the process. Besides, if I did more, I doubt I'd like it as much. And for me, *enjoying* exercise is as important as anything else.

So do enough but not too much. The important thing is to do what's appropriate for *you*—not for your friend or your mate or your coach, whether the coach be a person or a book, like this one.

If the programs in this book don't work for you, modify them so they do; that's the approach I've taken all the way through. Balance. Find the golden mean that works for you.

Balanced PaceWalking

Can PaceWalkers overdo it too? You bet they can. Balance is as important in PaceWalking as it is in any other aerobic activity. With the low level of musculoskeletal stress in PaceWalking, overuse injuries are rare, but it's just as possible for PaceWalkers to spend too much time at their sport as it is for any other athlete to do so. More than three hours of PaceWalking per week will probably not afford you increased health benefits, nor will more than eight to ten hours a week make you any more fit. What it may do, however, is afford you more injuries.

In this case, though, the injuries might well be psychological rather than physical. Health involves a state of well-being, so how you *feel* about what you're doing can be as important as any other aspect of your condition. And if doing too much PaceWalking has made the activity a trial rather than a pleasure, contributing to that scourge of anyone who exercises—burn-out—well, so much for well-being.

Decide what it is that you want out of PaceWalking and set out to accomplish it, and no more. The sport should help you manage stress, not add to it. Balance, balance. It's the key to success in any aerobic sport, the key to managing injury and realizing the greatest health and fitness benefits possible.

Health and Fitness

The focus of PaceWalking is primarily health, not fitness. There's a difference. Health is a state of well-being, of optimum functioning, of the absence of disease, and of the control of both external and internal risk factors. Fitness is the ability to do physical work over time. Believe it or not, you can be fit without being healthy. Everyone knows hard-working exercisers who are often sick or irritable. Everyone knows exercisers who smoke or drink immoderately. These people may be fit, but they're not healthy. Perhaps the best examples are drug-using athletes who are superfit and accomplish a high level of physical activity while systematically abusing their bodies and ruining their health.

Conversely, good health requires fitness, but only to a moderate level. As we've seen, at a certain point in your exercise, somewhere in the midrange of the fitness scale, you've received as much health benefit as you're going to get. Although increasing the amount of exercise may make you more fit, it probably won't make you healthier.

So it all depends on what you want out of your exercise. As I have said repeatedly, it's very important to set goals. In endurance sports such as PaceWalking, running, and cycling, fitness beyond what's necessary for good health is important only if you want to win races. When I talk about racing for PaceWalkers, I do so only in terms of participation and finishing. And I talk about those races of a length reasonable to tackle based on three hours of aerobic exercise per week. Primarily what PaceWalkers are after is health, not a high level of fitness.

Therefore PaceWalking, or any healthful exercise, should be undertaken as part of a comprehensive effort aimed at good health. The strategy should include not smoking cigarettes or using smokeless tobacco, controlling drug and alcohol intake, keeping weight to a healthful level, reducing the amount of fat in your diet, managing stress, and being cautious—wearing a seat belt, for example. Without such an overall effort, exercise by itself can't help you much. It's not a cure-all. It's a useful tool that can ensure lasting benefits if done in conjunction with other healthful measures.

Exercise not only complements such efforts, but it also helps accomplish them. For example, exercising can help you give up smoking; it's used for just that purpose in some formal smoking intervention programs. And exercise completely eliminates another, not-so-obvious risk factor. If you do any exercise at all you no longer have to worry about one of the greatest stumbling blocks to good health: lack of exercise. (In fact, Los Angeles pathologist Thomas Bassler has come up with a wonderful piece of advice for the nonexerciser. Nonexercisers should definitely undergo a complete medical examination including blood analysis for cholesterol and triglyceride levels and a treadmill cardiac-stress test. He says they have to make sure that they're healthy enough to withstand the strain of *not exercising.*)

The Health Benefits of Exercise

Exercise can only go so far in altering the hand that heredity has dealt us. If you don't have the genetic codes of an Arnold Schwarzenneger or a Jane Fonda, you won't become like them no matter how much you work out. But exercise can help you make the most of what you've got.

In terms of health, that means that exercise can help make your heart pump as efficiently as possible. That's important. The heart is a wondrous pump. It beats an average of seventy-two times every minute of our lives, making sure blood gets to every nook and cranny of the body. It requires no conscious upkeep, no periodic tune-ups. It just keeps beating away. Until it breaks down, that is. Heart disease is the foremost killer in the United States. When the pump is no longer able to supply the body with life-sustaining blood, life ceases.

So anything that makes the heart stronger and more efficient is good for you. Exercise does just that. By being consistently forced to beat at a reasonably high rate for a reasonable length of time, the heart strengthens and develops the ability to pump more blood per beat. In physiological language, this latter characteristic is called increased stroke volume. Not only does the heart beat more powerfully, but it's able to pump fewer times per minute to meet the body's need for blood. That's good. The most obvious result of this increased pumping power is a slower resting heart rate.

Although no one knows for sure, it's possible that a decreased resting heart rate accounts for the increased life expectancy regular exercisers enjoy (more on that later). If the healthy heart is capable of just so many beats before wearing out, it stands to reason that, if it beats less to accomplish the same amount of work, it will last longer.

More immediately, you'll notice this increasingly efficient heart capability because you'll have to work harder to push your heart into the aerobic range. As your body's cardiovascular system becomes more efficient, it accomplishes tasks more easily. And when you stop pushing, your heart will return to its resting rate more quickly than before. You'll find yourself out of breath less often and relaxed more often. I just can't say too many good things about the effect of exercise on your heart and cardiovascular system.

Exercise and the Prevention of Heart Disease

There are many studies on the subject of exercise and its relation to heart disease. Research by Dr. Ralph Paffenbarger of Stanford Medical School, generally considered to be the most authoritative on the subject, reinforces the findings of Dr. David Siscovick of the University of North Carolina Medical School and many other people as well. The evidence is clear that regular aerobic exercise, in the range of one to three hours per week, reduces the risk of heart attack by about *half*, compared to the risk of not exercising at all. And this reduced rate still holds while taking into account other heart attack risk factors such as cigarette smoking, hypertension, and family history. Exercise is one of the most effective strategies possible to reduce the likelihood of a heart attack.

The reasons are many. For example, exercise has a marvelous influence on the notorious character that lurks in the blood of all of us—cholesterol. Actually, not all cholesterol is bad. There are two types: heavy cholesterol, or high-density lipoprotein (HDL, for short); and light cholesterol, or low-density lipoprotein (LDL). It's the LDL that contributes to the buildup of harmful deposits along the walls of our arteries as we grow older. That accumulation of these deposits leads to a disease called atherosclerosis, which can cause potentially harmful interruptions of the blood supply to the heart and the brain. It's this interrupted blood flow that can lead to heart attacks and strokes. HDL, on the other hand, seems to work something like an arterial vacuum cleaner. It prevents the accumulation of harmful substances and actually seems to remove some of it when it does appear.

The effect of exercise on cholesterol is entirely salutary: It lowers levels of harmful LDL and raises levels of beneficial HDL. The evidence comes from many quarters, not the least of those being animal studies. In one experiment a group of monkeys was fed a high-fat diet designed to produce atherosclerosis. Half the monkeys were trained to exercise regularly on a treadmill and were tested to make sure that they achieved an aerobic effect, while the other half did nothing in particular in the way of aerobic exercise. At the end of the study the exercising monkeys had high levels of beneficial HDL, low levels of harmful LDL, and no demonstrable heart disease, even though they had been eating a high-fat diet. But the nonexercising monkeys were in bad shape, showing evidence of severe heart disease and atherosclerosis.

Furthermore, exercise decreases the level of the triglycerides, another harmful group of fatty substances known to be related to atherosclerosis. And exercise improves the body's ability to dissolve blood clots that can form on little rough places in the arterial walls, further reducing the risk of atherosclerosis.

Sudden Death and Exercise

Sudden death from heart disease in regular exercisers is a very rare event. Regular exercise tends to protect people against cardiac arrest. Again, while David Siscovick's study suggested that exercisers are five times more likely to die suddenly when exercising than they are when resting, it also showed that nonexercisers are fifty-six times more likely to die during exercise than they are when resting. And, of course, their overall risk of dying from a heart attack is about twice that of exercisers. When something as common as shoveling snow can be enough to cause a heart attack in a nonexerciser, it would seem wise to do something to avert such a possibility.

Still, the question of what actually causes the sudden deaths of well-conditioned exercisers is a controversial one. There are only a few of these incidents every year, but they do attract attention, especially when the deceased is Jim Fixx, the running writer, or John Kelly, the Olympic oarsman.

Pathologist Thomas Bassler has an intriguing theory concerning the problem. He points out that most of the runners who die while running show no evidence of atherosclerosis. It's likely, then, that something other than heart attack must be killing them. What might that be? Well, most such runners are well conditioned but very thin. They often follow very limited diets, low in calories and nutritients like vitamins, protein, and necessary fat. What kills them, Bassler suggests, is a combination of not eating properly, being too thin, and training too much—all of which can induce the heart to beat irregularly. These people die, reasons Bassler, of a fatal cardiac arrhythmia—a heart that, in effect, skips a beat or beats so fast that it cannot pump blood.

So we return, from a different direction, to the necessity of balance. Bassler recommends that exercisers eat a balanced diet that includes ample foods from all food groups. I agree (see the next chapter, Nutrition and Weight Control for the PaceWalker). And I would add that sudden death in exercising exercisers, rare though it may be, is a testament to the need for a balanced approach to working out. Our bodies simply don't like being forced too far in any one direction. Sooner or later one way or another, they rebel.

The Jim Fixx Syndrome

Jim Fixx, author of *The Complete Book of Running,* was one of the most important popularizers of running for exercise during the sport's rapid growth in the 1970s. He died while on a run in rural Vermont on July 20, 1984. The cause of his death was probably cardiac arrhythmia. But there ends the similarity of his death to those of the few others who also died while exercising. For Jim Fixx had serious atherosclerotic heart disease. His fatal irregular heart beat was probably the result of his heart disease, not of eating badly or of being underweight, neither of which pertained to him. But in Jim Fixx's case, it's likely that running actually added years to his life rather than shortened it.

Fixx had a history that pointed him in the direction of heart attack. His father died of one in his early forties. Before Fixx became a runner in his late thirties, he had been an overweight, out-of-shape, heavy cigarette smoker. And he worked in the high-stress world of advertising. Even after he began running, lost a great deal of weight, and stopped smoking, Fixx continued to work in advertising. He was an obvious candidate for coronary artery disease, running or not.

The real sadness surrounding Fixx's death is that in the last months of his life he experienced warning signs of impending trouble and he ignored them. He had occasional chest pains when he exerted himself, a sure tip-off for heart trouble. His friends knew that he had been having complaints and tried to get him to undergo a medical evaluation, but Fixx refused. In effect, he left himself to his fate. And with his history, there was little doubt what it would be. The only question was, when would it happen?

If Fixx had gone for testing, it's likely that his heart disease would have been detected. He could have been treated, either with diet and medication or, depending on the severity of his case, coronary artery bypass surgery. In that case, he probably would be with us today. But Fixx was afflicted with what Ken Cooper describes as the Jim Fixx Syndrome: the belief that an aerobic exerciser is impervious to heart disease.

Any aerobic exercise significantly lowers a person's risk of having arteriosclerotic heart disease and of dying from a heart attack. Sudden death from heart attack is extremely rare in regular aerobic exercisers who are of normal weight and eat a balanced diet. Aerobic exercise will not cure all ills, however. You still have to take care of yourself. Listen to your body, and if in doubt, see a doctor. Those are the two things Jim Fixx failed to do.

Exercise and Cardiac Rehabilitation

Aerobic exercise not only decreases the risk of heart disease, but when carefully planned, monitored, and controlled, it can also help to rehabilitate people who have suffered heart attacks. Exercise does double duty: It can prevent and it can treat disease. There are very few strategies that can make that claim!

PaceWalking is an ideal choice for an aerobic exercise to be used in rehabilitation. It requires no special skills, is easy on the body, is enjoyable to do, and gives as complete an aerobic workout as any other activity. It's especially good for older people, since it's the most gentle of aerobic activities. If you're a recovering heart-attack sufferer, and your doctor hasn't recommended PaceWalking, you might suggest it yourself. I suspect you'll receive an enthusiastic okay. In the beginning, however, it's a good idea to do it under the supervision of a regular cardiac rehabilitation program. Many hospitals have them these days.

Exercise and the Prevention of Noncardiovascular Disease

One can almost forget, in the excitement of chronicling the utility of exercise in preventing and treating heart disease, that there are other things going on in the body. Not to worry. Exercise is useful in dealing with them, too.

For example, exercise against gravity—that is, virtually any activity except swimming, in which gravity is essentially neutralized—increases bone density. Bone is not static. Nor is it dead. It waxes and wanes just like anything else in the body. When bone is subjected to stress, such as to the pounding of running, it builds up to handle the increased demands. When there is relatively little required of it, as in nonexercising, it remains as is or even atrophies. A dramatic example of bone atrophy is the experience of astronauts who, after an extended time in weightless space, lost so much bone mass and density that upon their return to earth they were unable even to stand; see chapter 5 for more on that. Here, too, balance is important. Too much stress can break bones down. Too little can cause harmful atrophy. PaceWalking provides an ideal balance for building strong bones.

Because of its ability to increase bone density, exercising against gravity is one of the best preventive measures you can take to reduce the risk of osteoporosis. This disease, which softens bones and decreases density, is particularly common in women. These days, calcium supplements are touted as a good preventive measure for osteoporosis, and such may indeed be the case. But it's not yet clear just how dietary calcium affects the development of the disease. So exercise is most likely the best thing you can do to ward off osteoporosis.

When not overdone, exercise is not only *not* bad for joints, but it's actually good for them. As with most everything else in your body, if you don't use it you lose it. As health and science writer Jane Brody has pointed out, among Americans, joints don't wear out, they rust out. But, once again, balance is important.

If you do suffer an acute joint injury, exercise is absolutely essential if you're to recover from the injury. In fact, in some cases, exercise—in the form of muscle stretching and strengthening as well as aerobic exercise—may be the only way to recover. If you should suffer a serious joint injury, consult a doctor who will set up a good rehabilitation program. And if exercise isn't a central part of that program, it may be time to look for another physician.

PaceWalking is a particularly good sport for people who have suffered ankle, knee, or hip injuries. It gives the muscles surrounding those joints a healthy workout while minimizing the stress the joints must undergo. As an example, I broke my ankle running on an icy day in February 1982. With the help of a strengthening and stretching program and regular exercise, I haven't had any problems with the ankle since. I don't expect to, either.

Obesity is another problem that exercise can help overcome. The combination of exercise and diet is unequaled as a strategy for losing weight. Diet alone is not nearly as effective as when in concert with exercise, since aerobic exercise makes the body use energy more efficiently. Over time it actually changes your metabolism so that you tend to use accumulated fat for energy. Be suspicious of any diet that promises to reduce weight without exercise. (More on all that in the next chapter.)

Exercise helps reduce blood pressure. It increases the lungs' ability to take in oxygen and improves oxygen uptake in the muscles. Exercise is helpful in dealing with diabetes, too. The reasons probably involve exercise's ability to control obesity, which aggravates diabetes. Body fat interferes with the action of insulin, the hormone that controls blood-sugar levels. Exercise helps make the body's tissues more sensitive to insulin. And exercise may reduce the risk of certain forms of cancer, such as cancer of the colon, and breast and reproductive system cancer in women. Just why exercise may be effective in combating some cancers isn't yet clear, but it may be the direct result of exercise stimulating the body's production of its own anticancer mechanisms, or the indirect result of a reduction in smoking and of eating a diet low in fats, which often accompany a regular exercise program.

Last, but certainly not least, exercise seems to improve the sex life. I admit that this may be a subjective judgment, but many exercisers report it to be true. People who exercise regularly tend to look better, feel better, and generally be sexier. Of course overtraining can lead to fatigue, and fatigue can lead to a decline in one's interest in sex. Once again, balance is the thing. And, in contrast to the opinion of some people, sex before exercise does not reduce the quality of your workout. You used to hear of professional boxers sequestering themselves from the opposite sex before their fights, in the belief that sex might reduce their fighting energy. But there's no evidence to support that view. As Casey Stengel once said, it's not sex that hurts your performance, it's the energy you use trying to catch up with people to have sex with that hurts you.

But, sad to say, even though sex causes our hearts to beat well into the aerobic range for a few minutes, it doesn't offer aerobic benefits. Nor does it burn up many calories. It's only the increased heart rate caused by the rhythmic contraction of *major* muscle groups that results in significant calorie consumption.

Exercise, Longevity, and Life Expectancy

The Bible says that our years on this earth are three score and ten. Today, despite all our scientific advances, not much has changed. Our time still measures in the range of seventy years or so. What has changed is that many more people are reaching that age. So although our longevity may not be much greater than it ever has been, our life expectancy, the chance of getting to be seventy plus, has increased—that is, more people are living to be "old."

It's been the advances in nutrition, public health, and medicine over the last three centuries that have allowed more people to live their allotted span. Diseases that used to kill people early, especially in the first year of life, have largely been eliminated. Now more people are surviving that precarious first year to be able to live to be "old." So when we say that life expectancy is going up, we don't mean that our potential life span is much longer than it used to be, but that more people are reaching it.

The distinction is important to understand when looking at research on the relationship between exercise and aging. For example, in a study done on Harvard College alumni, Ralph Paffenbarger and his colleagues have found that regular aerobic exercise for two to three hours per week increases life expectancy by about two years. In other words, if you exercise regularly, you're likely to add two years to your life.

And what's more, you'll live those advanced years with a degree of youthfulness and vitality unknown to earlier times. An increasing number of people look and feel younger at seventy than ever before. Not only has our life expectancy increased, so has the quality of our life along the way. And, again, the reasons are exercise, improved nutrition, and better health practices.

So we find ourselves, as never before, blessed with the possibility of living out our years as fully as possible. The choice is ours—the tools are in our hands. And foremost among them is exercise.

In the words of the seventeenth-century English poet John Dryden,

> Better to hunt in Fields, for Health unbought,
> Than fee the Doctor for a nauseous Draught.
> The Wise, for Cure, on exercise depend;
> God never made his Work, for Man to mend.

CHAPTER 10

Nutrition and Weight Control for the PaceWalker

*I*n 1978 I worked with a group of students to plan a course on nutrition that, we hoped, would be required of all students at the medical school where I teach. There was no required nutrition course then; unfortunately, there still isn't. But that effort of ten years ago taught me a lot.

Even as a specialist in preventive medicine, I knew little about nutrition. It hadn't been touched upon in my med school training or in my preventive medicine residency program. But then again, very few medical schools did—or still do—any serious teaching on the subject. That's the principal reason why so few doctors know much about nutrition. And that, in turn, is one reason why books and articles on various aspects of nutrition, especially on losing weight, are a staple on the lists of book publishers and in the pages of magazines. Most people have nowhere else to turn for nutritional advice. All of which is truly an amazing state of affairs, because good nutrition is so vitally important for good health and well-being.

Since that first exposure to the field of nutrition, I've learned much about it that has been useful, both professionally and personally. I've gradually changed my eating habits. And since I've become a regular exerciser, I've come to see how inextricably linked exercise and nutrition are. This connection shouldn't come as a surprise, but so many people, in both the health professions and the general public, seem to be unaware of it. The relationship is especially apparent if you think of life as motion.

Life as Motion

Life *is* motion. Motion of the muscles that we consciously control, as in the arms and legs. Motion of the muscles that we don't consciously control, as in the heart and digestive tract. Motion of the microelectrical currents in the brain. These motions regulate all voluntary and involuntary muscles, mediate all senses, and are the basis of thought, feelings, emotions, creativity. When these motions stop, life stops.

But none of these motions can take place without energy to fuel them. And energy comes from the food we eat. The magic word *calorie* is a measure of that energy or, more precisely, of the heat that's created when the body converts food into energy. We talk about eating so many calories per day, but what we're really talking about is how much heat the process of energy conversion is producing—that is, how much of a supply of potential energy we're consuming. The idea is to consume as much energy as we need, not any less or any more. If we eat too little, the body must get its necessary energy from somewhere else. Usually it draws what it needs from its own tissues, converting flesh into energy; that means we lose weight. If we eat too much, the body doesn't waste the extra energy, discarding it like gasoline overflowing a full tank. Rather it takes it in and for the most part converts it into extra tissue, usually fat, saving it for possible future use.

Exercise adds another dimension to the process. When you exercise, you force your body into *extra* motion. That requires extra energy. And the energy must come from somewhere. There are two possible sources: extra food, or the potential energy your body has already stored in the form of fat. To exercise either you must eat more or, if you don't, your body must tap its own reserves. In the latter case, your weight will decrease as your amount of exercise increases. It will decrease slowly, but it *will* decrease. That's either good news or bad news, depending on your point of view. Since the body's extra potential energy is stored mainly as fat, you'll burn off that fat as you exercise. For many people, that's a great pleasure. Furthermore, if you exercise enough to build up muscle, you can actually lose fat, gain weight by adding muscle, and look thinner, all at the same time. But if you're low in body fat to begin with, you can actually lose muscle by exercising. Again, the energy must come from somewhere, and if fat's not available the body will break down muscle. That's not so good. For people in this boat, good nutrition is especially important.

So it all comes back to the link between motion and energy—in other words, life and food. To be healthy, you have to eat healthfully. Exercise and nutrition are two sides of the same coin.

Nutrition and Balance

Just as balance is important in the kind, duration, and intensity of the exercise you do, likewise it's the key to eating properly. The body's inclination to stay in equilibrium, the homeostasis I talked about in the last chapter, works for nutrition as it does for everything else. Too much food is not good; too little food is not good.

For example, overexercising may eventually lead to injury, while lack of exercise increases your risk of all sorts of serious problems, such as heart disease. If you eat too much, you'll start accumulating unnecessary fat. If you eat too little, you'll eventually burn up the body's normal fat supply and start using up muscle tissue to supply energy. That's the state of starvation.

In our country, starvation is rare (although, unfortunately, hunger is not). Vitamin and mineral deficiency is also rare, although you'd never know it to look at the time and money devoted to selling people supplemental vitamins. But we do face two major nutritional problems, both arising from ignorance about nutrition and from not eating a balanced diet. One problem is obesity. (There are 12 to 20 million obese people in this country, not to mention others who are simply somewhat overweight. There are 50 million overweight women alone [see page 190 for the definitions of obesity and overweight.]) The other problem is too much fat and cholesterol in the blood.

Should you have either or both of these problems, you can probably deal with them by exercising and eating in a balanced way. It's rarely necessary to do anything drastic. In fact, drastic measures, and there are a lot of them out there, almost invariably lead to long-term failure. They may have some immediate positive effects, but most of the time you eventually end up right back where you started, or worse off. Most fad diets based on quick weight-loss gimmicks are detrimental to health and fitness.

Later in this chapter I'll discuss quick weight-loss diets and the problems of obesity and high fat and cholesterol in the blood. But first let's look at a good, all-purpose nutrition plan.

The American Heart Association Diet

My favorite way to a balanced diet is the American Heart Association (AHA) plan. In the average American diet, more than 40 percent of the calories come from eating fat. With the AHA diet, that figure is reduced to around 30 percent, a level that is considered healthy for the heart and for the body as a whole. The AHA diet supplies about 15 percent of its calories in the form of protein and 55 percent in the form of carbohydrates. It's a well-balanced, healthy, palatable diet.

Some goals of the AHA diet include lowering so-called saturated fat intake in the diet ("saturated fat," a biochemical term describing molecular structure, is fat that is usually solid at room temperature. It can contribute to the development of atherosclerosis), increasing the intake of unsaturated fat (the liquid food fat that may help to reduce the incidence of atherosclerosis), and meeting all other normal nutritional needs.

The basics of the AHA diet are straightforward, sensible, and logical. The diet separates food into four groups: (1) green vegetables and fruits; (2) milk products; (3) breads, cereals, and starchy vegetables; (4) meat, poultry, fish, and other high-protein food. To achieve a balanced diet, you should eat something from each of these groups every day. To reduce your fat intake, eat more fresh fruits and vegetables and less whole-milk based products. Eat more chicken and fish (but remember to remove the chicken skin. With its skin, especially when deep-fried, chicken is fattier than a good piece of lean beef). Cut down on beef, and avoid other fatty meats. Breads and pastas are fine, but avoid egg-based breads. Eat no more than two eggs per week. And when you use vegetable oils, choose polyunsaturated ones. In particular, avoid coconut and palm oils.

If this approach involves changes in your diet, you can make them gradually, almost imperceptibly. Say that you eat beef three times a week. You don't have to go "cold turkey" (although cold turkey is a good substitute—without the skin, of course); just cut down to twice a week to start, then down to once a week, and so on until finally you're only eating beef a couple of times a month or whatever is comfortable for you. If you're used to a couple of eggs for breakfast daily, cut down to a couple of eggs every other day, then every third day, and so on. Fill in the blanks with fruit, bread, cereals, and fruit juices. Eat frozen low-fat yogurt instead of ice cream. Snack on carrot and celery sticks rather than cheese and crackers. You can substitute mozzarella cheese, which is lower in fat, for cheddar. That's the way I did it, I now eat very little chocolate, which I used to guzzle, and no longer give the Cookie Monster a run for his money. But I got there gradually, little by little, bit by bit. And believe me, now when I occasionally have that juicy steak or hot fudge sundae, does it taste good! Much better, in fact, than it ever tasted when I was eating it all the time.

Conspicuous for its absence here is a detailed daily diet schedule, similar to those included in various diet books. It's a conscious omission. Given the general guidelines I've just presented and an understanding of the process of nutrition, which is the essence of this chapter, people who truly want to eat a healthful, balanced diet can devise their own.

The key is wanting to—not for your mate, or your friends, or your family, but for *yourself.* Good, healthful eating, whether you're overweight or not, requires a long-term commitment—as does PaceWalking or anything else in life that's worthwhile. And the only way you're going to make that commitment is if you decide to do it for yourself.

Here's the address of the AHA. They'll be happy to send you a free copy of their diet and other related nutritional material. There's no better time to start than now:

> AMERICAN HEART ASSOCIATION
> 7320 Greenville Avenue
> Dallas, Texas 75231

Dietary Fiber

Eat lots of fiber—that's one of the slogans of modern good nutrition. Actually, in slightly different terms, it was one of the slogans of good nutrition in the nineteenth century, too. Graham crackers, for example, were invented in the American Midwest around 1840 by one Sylvester Graham. Made of whole-wheat flour, which we now know to be an excellent source of dietary fiber, graham crackers were intended to "improve the digestion" and help "purge the system." Among other things, dietary fiber does just that. (However, I doubt that chocolate-pudding graham-cracker pie was one of the uses old Mr. Graham had in mind when he developed his cracker. I may no longer eat much chocolate, but that doesn't mean I can't think about it.)

Fiber has several benefits. It helps speed the movement of digested food through the colon. It provides bulk, which helps elimination and helps prevent constipation. It absorbs up to 10 percent of the fat that you eat before it's digested. And it may absorb certain other potentially harmful substances, including some which may cause cancer.

Because of these characteristics, fiber is thought to be helpful in reducing the risk of intestinal diverticulitis, a disease that produces inflammed pockets along the wall of the colon; appendicitis; and cancer of the colon. It may be useful in the treatment of diabetes and atherosclerosis. It will certainly help you lose weight. Although fiber is included in calorie counts, it isn't completely digested and so actually supplies very few calories to your body.

Many different foods are good sources of fiber. In terms of percent fiber by weight, the best sources are high-fiber cereals containing 10 to 30 percent fiber. Wheat and oat bran are another good source. Vegetables and fruits are another source, although their levels are lower than those in cereals—generally 1 to 3 percent. These include corn, carrots, broccoli, peas, potatoes (with the skin), yams (one of my favorites—try them baked), dried peas, and beans, peaches, apples, strawberries, raspberries, blueberries, blackberries, and dried fruits, all eaten with seeds and skin. And, of course, there's whole-grain bread, which is about 10 percent fiber by weight.

The National Cancer Institute recommends that you eat 25 to 40 grams of *dietary* fiber per day. Many foods now list fiber content on their labels. Always look for the *dietary* fiber number, not the *crude* fiber number, which is usually quite a bit lower. You don't want to eat too much fiber, either. Like anything else, too much fiber can be harmful. For those who don't like to spend their time weighing and counting, I suggest half a cup to a cup of high-fiber cereal per day, plus an increased amount of fruits and vegetables. If you don't like the taste of high-fiber cereals, just put a lot of good high-fiber fruit on top.

Vitamin Supplements

Vitamins are a multibillion dollar industry in our country. But did you know that many of those dollars are literally flushed down the toilet? Most people's bodies have no use for excess vitamins or minerals in amounts above those established by the National Academy of Sciences as the Recommended Daily Allowances (RDAs). As stated in guidelines on vitamin supplementation issued by the American Dietetic Association, the American Institute of Nutrition, and the American Society for Clinical Nutrition most people satisfy the RDAs, which vary by age and sex, by eating an AHA-type balanced diet. If they take supplemental vitamins as well, some of the extra just goes right out in the urine and other wastes. But the body has no way to get rid of certain vitamins that it doesn't need; those it just stores up. For example, if the buildup of vitamins A and D becomes too large, it can actually be harmful. Too much vitamin D can lead to kidney stones, and too much vitamin A can actually cause you to lose your appetite, have itchy skin, and lose your hair.

It's not true that the foods we buy are vitamin depleted for one reason or another. Nor is it true that vitamins will give us extra energy. Energy comes from calories, which vitamins don't provide. Very large, so-called megadoses have not been shown by any scientific studies to improve health. The only time you need to take vitamin supplements is when you have been diagnosed by a physician or a nutritionist as having a specific vitamin deficiency, a very unusual occurrence in this country. The same applies to minerals such as iron. If the level of iron in your blood has been diagnosed as being low, then you need to take an iron supplement. But if your blood iron level is normal, taking additional iron may actually harm you.

To make sure you have enough vitamins and minerals, all you have to do is eat a balanced diet each day. And that's not difficult to do. In particular, eat plenty of dark, leafy green vegetables and bright yellow vegetables. Second, eat some dairy products each day, preferably of the low-fat variety. Third, eat some lean meat or chicken or fish on a regular basis. Fourth, eat citrus fruits or to- matoes or berries. And last, eat some whole-grain bread or cereal products, including pasta or other starchy foods. In other words, eat something from each of the four food groups each day, keep your fat level low, and don't eat more than you need. It's amazing how a balanced diet satisfies our needs in every area, and how simple it is to maintain one once you put your mind to it.

Obesity—What is it?

Don't eat more than you need. The words bear repeating, for one of the obvious consequences of overeating is obesity. Obesity describes a condition of being grossly overweight. But how much weight is too much? It's a question that is not easy to answer.

For many years the Metropolitan Life Insurance Company has published tables of what are considered "normal" weight by sex, height, and body build. For example, the normal weight for a 5'10" male of medium build, including 5 pounds of clothing, is 151 to 163 pounds. For a 5'5" woman of medium build wearing 3 pounds of clothing, normal weight is 127 to 141 pounds. It's generally be- lieved by most medical authorities that any weight up to 20 percent above the upper limit does not increase the risk of such problems as high blood pressure, diabetes, and, possibly, heart disease—in other words, those risks associated with obesity. So if you're a 5'5" woman, you may weigh up to 170 pounds and still not be obese, as far as health risks are concerned. Any more than 20 percent above your normal weight, and you fall into the increased risk category. Then you might well consider yourself obese.

That's one way of determining obesity. Another has to do with proportion of body fat. It's actually possible to be obese while not weighing any more than is normal for your sex, height, and body build. It's not absolutely clear how much of a risk factor a high body-fat proportion is, but it is clear that excess fat is not healthy, even if your weight is no more than 20 percent above what's normal for you.

For example, I had a complete body-fat evaluation done in 1981, a year after I started exercising regularly. I found that even though I weighed only 15 pounds more than my normal weight of 165 pounds—that's less than 10 percent above where I should've been—I had 22 percent body fat. The normal body-fat range for males is 13 to 18 percent, for women 20 to 25 percent. My proportion of body fat was much higher than it should have been. Although I wasn't significantly overweight, by body-fat standards I was obese.

What constitutes obesity then, starts to look a little more complex than being just a matter of pounds. It has to do in part with weight and in part with what that weight consists of. According to the Metropolitan Life tables, a 6'4" man with a large frame should weigh between 181 and 207 pounds. Does that mean that a 6'4" football linebacker who weighs 250 pounds is obese? He's more than 20 percent over normal limits. But he has only 12 to 13 percent body fat, which is not unusual for a well-trained athlete, and much of his weight is in muscle. No, this man is neither obese nor, for him, overweight.

This same kind of analysis can apply to the rest of us, as well. In the late 1970s, I weighed close to 190 pounds. By beginning to eat a more balanced, lower-calorie diet, I got my weight down to around 180—with, however, that 22 percent body-fat proportion. My waist was close to 40 inches. When I began exercising regularly in 1980, my weight soon dropped to about 175 pounds. Since then I've continued to exercise—PaceWalking, running, cycling, swimming, and doing some weight lifting in the winters. And over that time my weight has actually climbed back up to around 180 pounds. However, my body fat has dropped to 17 percent and my waist to 37 inches. What a pleasure it is to walk into the cleaners with a bunch of trousers and say, "Take 'em in."

Am I obese? No. My weight is still about 10 percent above what the table says it should be for my sex, height, and body build. But my proportion of body fat has dropped to within an acceptable range. And although I've gained weight over the years, it's been in the form of muscle rather than fat, which I've actually lost. Even though I'm heavier, people tell me I look thinner. And, of course, I've also lowered my risk of heart disease and high blood pressure and the other problems associated with obesity.

In my view, and it is certainly not shared by everyone, there are two other components of obesity: how you look and how you feel. Just as with exercise and eating, proper weight is determined in part by what *feels* right. If I went on a calorie-restricted diet I could get my weight down below 170 pounds, but I know I would look and feel terrible. In the summer of 1985, I was training hard for two long triathlons, and I got my weight down to 173 pounds. I felt great when I got on the scale, but I didn't feel too great otherwise. I became dizzy when I did nothing more than arise from a kneeling position, not to mention trying to stay on a bike for long periods of time. I just wasn't eating enough. I went back to a more substantial diet, gained weight, and soon I felt fine. (Body fat does have its pluses, by the way, as long as you don't have too much of it. For one thing, it helps keep wrinkles down by smoothing out your skin. For another, it's a great insulator in cold water. In a number of triathlons I've been happy as a clam in water from which skinny people were being pulled right and left. And body fat gives you extra buoyancy, a real plus in long swims.)

So obesity is a combination of how much you weigh, how much body fat you have, and how you look and feel. The number on the bathroom scale just doesn't tell the whole story—and scales are not always consistent from day to day, anyway. You can sometimes get a better idea of weight simply by how your clothes fit. You have to weigh the pluses and minuses and decide what combination is right for you. Just remember to balance all things. Compulsive undereating is as harmful as compulsive overeating. And remember that you can actually *look* thinner and be healthier, without losing weight, by exercising to reduce your proportion of body fat and build up muscle. It all depends on what's right for you.

What to Do About Obesity

In most cases, the answer to obesity is simple: Eat appropriately and exercise. But to apply that formula to your situation, you must first determine which category of obesity you fall into.

For example, there is the most familiar kind of obesity—the fat person who eats a lot. There is the obesity associated with pregnancy, in which gaining weight is part of the normal course of things. There is the kind of obesity that you inherit, no matter what you eat. And there is the obesity of people who don't eat much at all. Their weight tends to hold fairly steady, even if they eat a low-calorie diet. It's hard for them to lose weight because they already eat so little that they don't have much to cut back on.

If you are obese, to determine what category you're in, first pick up a food calorie chart. You can find them in many supermarkets, at your doctor's or nutritionist's office, or at a bookstore. Keep a detailed three-day record of everything you eat. Then tally up the calories you've consumed and see where you fit. The average woman needs between 1,800 and 2,000 calories per day to maintain weight, while the average man needs between 2,400 to 2,700 calories. If you're puzzled, see a nutritionist. You can locate one in the Yellow Pages or at your local hospital. Or find one of the relatively few doctors who know something about nutrition. One way or another, you'll find out whether you need to exercise to lose weight or to combine exercise with a lower calorie diet. (More on this below.)

The next step is the most important of all: You must decide if you want to do something about your obesity—*really* want to. For being obese is no sin. It may mean increased risk of disease and other problems, but this is a free country, and obesity is not a moral issue, as some would make it out to be. All of us have the right to decide if we're willing to shoulder those risks or not; for reasons of looks, or comfort, or just plain inertia you may decide to stay the way you are. It's important to know where you stand, for when it comes to obesity there are no quick fixes or miracle cures. Successfully dealing with obesity requires a long-term commitment. You have to want to, and want to badly.

Weight Loss for Overeaters

If you're one of those people who consume too many calories, the strategy is simple. First, begin eating more intelligently, more healthfully. Cut down on calories. Again, the AHA diet offers a fine course of action. Use your calorie charts to good purpose, and devise a well-balanced diet that affords you no more than the calories you need. Chances are you've been consuming far too many calories. What I'm suggesting is not easy. You've tried before, I'm sure. But have you ever combined a calorie-reduction diet that you've made up yourself with the second part of my program, exercise?

Chances are you haven't been doing much exercise. I think you'll find that the combination of healthful eating and healthful exercise is impossible to beat. Here's where the PaceWalking programs in chapter 4 are especially useful. Follow them regularly, eat well, and you'll notice pleasant changes sooner than you think.

And *stay* with your eating/exercise program. Even after you've lost the amount of weight you were aiming for, stay with it. A common problem with losing weight is that people quickly revert to their old life-style once they've achieved their weight-loss goals. The result? They balloon right back up to where they were. Not only is that frustrating, but gaining and losing weight time and time again isn't healthy. Once you've found your stride, stick with it.

Obesity and Pregnancy

If you're not careful, the natural weight gain that occurs during pregnancy can become exaggerated and remain with you long afterwards. And multiple pregnancies without weight control can cause women to become very heavy, indeed.

The antidotes are eating well and exercising. I suggest you refer back to chapter 6 for some specific suggestions for exercising. And for a healthful diet, consult your doctor or nutritionist. The AHA diet is certainly a good basis for pregnancy, but pregnant women should take special care with what they eat. As with anything concerning pregnancy, if in doubt consult your doctor.

Inherited Obesity and Low-Calorie Obesity

Several recent studies have shown that some people inherit their tendency to gain weight, no matter how little they eat. More common are the people who have no genetic predisposition to obesity but will tell you, "I eat next to nothing and *still* I can't lose weight." They're not lying. Often the problem is a result of frequently using quick weight-loss diets. You know what they are. They've been around for years, are constantly recycled and given new names by new authors and new publishers. They have some kind of dietary gimmick that enables you to drop a lot of weight very quickly. If you're more than 20 percent overweight, you might lose as much as twenty pounds in two weeks, maybe even more.

But these diets make little attempt to help you change your long-term eating habits or, much more important for low-calorie obesity, help you to become a regular exerciser. So you stick to the diet religiously for the prescribed fourteen or twenty-one days, lose weight, and then go right back to your old habits. And the weight goes right back on.

What's more, many people who use these diets actually end up heavier than they were before. Why? Because of the body's tendency to adjust what's called its energy thermostat up or down according to the demands made on it. Here's how it works. Our energy thermostat regulates the rate at which the body uses energy when it's not doing much of anything besides running its own support systems like circulation and breathing—it's called the resting metabolism rate. The average woman needs about 60 calories per hour, the average man about 80. When you start following a fast weight-reduction diet and drastically reduce the number of calories you take in, the body doesn't have time to draw on its fat for the extra energy it suddenly seems to need. To compensate, the body resets its energy thermostat, downwards. Remember that fat is the body's reserve energy source, your protection against the famine that might never come. Your body doesn't want to give up that protection easily, so instead it turns down the burner, reducing the resting metabolism rate to, say, 40 calories per hour for women and 50 calories per hour for men.

So far so good—at least it *seems* that way. You lose some weight and begin feeling pretty good about yourself. But soon enough you revert to your old eating habits and begin increasing the number of calories you consume once again. But your body does not automatically reset its energy thermostat upwards. Now your newly regulated body needs fewer calories to function. Where does the rush of calories go as you resume your old ways of eating? You guessed it, to fat. You regain the weight you lost and often more. You feel like a failure and blame the diet, for the wrong reasons as it turns out, and become a prime candidate for the next miracle weight-loss plan. And so it goes. Repeat the pattern often enough, and your weight may soar as a result. That's low-calorie obesity.

In the long run, there's only one way to deal with low-calorie obesity: Eat an AHA-type, low-fat, balanced diet and start exercising. The reasons are obvious. If you're already eating few calories, you can't cut many more out. If you do, you'll be inviting all sorts of protein-vitamin-mineral deficiencies. The only way that you'll lose weight is by making your fat go to work for you. You've simply got to start using up a portion of these energy reserves each day. How? By exercising.

Exercise allows you to use your energy reserves in two ways. First, the added energy demands of exercise will cause your body to dip into its reserves. That's why eating an appropriate diet is so important. Your diet should supply your normal, rather low calorie needs, but no more, so that exercise can tap the reserves. Second, if quick weight-loss dieting sets your energy thermostat downwards, exercising moves it back up. Soon your body will burn more calories than otherwise, even when you're not exercising.

Even if you only exercise a little, it's better than doing nothing. To attain an aerobic effect you must sustain an aerobic heart rate for a minimum of twenty minutes three times a week, but to lose weight, any exercise is helpful even if it is not aerobic. No matter how much you do, you're forcing your body to burn more calories than it would otherwise. So it's worth beginning to do some exercise, even if you don't follow with any regular plan.

For example, it may be enough at the beginning to use the stairs instead of the elevator when you go to work. You may want to walk the quarter mile to the convenience store instead of driving the car. You may want to swim a few laps in the pool instead of simply splashing around and playing with the kids. Or you may want to take a twenty-minute stroll after dinner. Just getting your body moving will do to get started.

Once you've begun to exercise, it may be time to turn to chapter 4 and the PaceWalking program. There is no exercise more accessible to the person trying to lose weight. The Introductory Program begins with ten minutes three times per week—what could be easier? And once you move your heart rate into the aerobic range, you'll start burning off about 10 calories per minute. Stay at it and eat a healthy diet, and you'll be more than pleased with the results. Who knows? You might get hooked on exercise, too. It's happened to the best, and least, of us.

CHAPTER 11

Conclusion

*P*aceWalking is a marvelous sport. It makes you feel good. It's good for your health. It's not hard to do. It produces little pain when you do it, unlike many other aerobic sports. At the same time, the benefits are commensurate with those of other aerobic sports done at the same level of intensity.

Exercise may be an entirely new part of your life, and PaceWalking may be the one sport that you will do. Or you may be substituting PaceWalking for other aerobic sports that have bored you or injured you. You may be adding PaceWalking to your aerobic sport repertoire. For whatever reason you are PaceWalking, setting a goal, as I have said repeatedly, is the first step you should take, even before the first step in your first PaceWalk.

Balance and gradual change are two other principles I have emphasized. However you use PaceWalking, if you want to make it a regular part of your life, for a long time, you should find the balance that fits you and suits your abilities, your inclinations, the way you live the rest of your life. PaceWalking should be an addition, not a subtraction, to your life. And the best way to reach this balanced state is gradually. There is no rush. You are much more likely to become a regular exerciser if you enter the sport slowly, building up your fitness level and your commitment steadily and carefully, than if you plunge in head first.

What does all of this really mean? It means taking control of your life. It means deciding for yourself that you are going to do something that will benefit you. But this thing that you are going to do—PaceWalk—is not easy. It is technically simple and it is virtually pain free, but it is not easy. There is no lazy-person's way to get in shape. There is no effortless road to weight loss.

To accomplish these goals you are going to have to take control of your life, of your schedule, of your eating. We are exposed to many nonhealthful stimuli in our society: huge advertising campaigns for alcoholic beverages and cigarettes; lots of foods filled with fats and sugars available in our supermarkets right alongside the healthful ones; fume-filled streets that can make regular aerobic exercise difficult; a medical system that stresses treatment of disease rather than prevention of illness and promotion of health; and few incentives or encouragement to exercise regularly. Surveys show that most people know exercise is good for them, but fewer than 25 percent actually do aerobic exercise on a regular basis.

It is easy to drift through life, letting outside forces dictate your behavior. It takes no effort *not* to exercise regularly; it takes quite a bit of effort to get yourself onto a regular exercise program. Once on such a program you'll wonder how you ever did without it. But even then, when it's cold or dark or you just plain don't feel like it, it still takes effort to do a scheduled workout.

All of this means taking control. It means scheduling. It means choosing your food with some care. It means opening new perspectives on life. It means getting in touch with feelings that you didn't know you had. It means developing physical abilities that you didn't know you possessed. It means becoming self-disciplined, perhaps in a way you never thought you could.

The prospect of taking control of their own lives, of becoming proactive instead of reactive, is scary to some people. But believe me; it is highly rewarding to almost everyone who tries it.

PaceWalking offers you the chance to take control of your body, to do good things for it, and to do good things for your mind. PaceWalking is fun. PaceWalking is simple. PaceWalking is not easy. But when you decide to become a PaceWalker, you will find that the rewards of the sport are manifold.

APPENDIX 1

Notes

Chapter 1: PaceWalking — An Introduction

"Protective Effect of Physical Activity on Coronary Heart Disease." *Morbidity and Mortality Weekly Report* 36 (July 10, 1987), p. 426.

George Sheehan, "Walking: The Best Exercise of All." *Physician and Sportsmedicine* (October 1986), p. 41.

Chapter 2: PaceWalking — The Roots of Success

Kenneth Cooper, *Running Without Fear*. New York: M. Evans and Co., 1985.

Chapter 3: How to PaceWalk

Kenneth Cooper, *Running Without Fear*. New York: M. Evans and Co., 1985.

James G. Garrick and Peter Radetsky, *Peak Condition: Winning Strategies to Prevent, Treat, and Rehabilitate Sports Injuries*. New York: Perennial Library/Harper & Row Publishers, 1988.

Chapter 4: The PaceWalking Program

Kenneth Cooper, *Running Without Fear*. New York: M. Evans and Co., 1985.

H. Higdon, "High Success on Low Mileage." *The Runner* (March 1987), p. 40.

Chris Walsh, *The Bowerman System*. Los Altos, Calif.: Tafnews Press, 1983.

Chapter 5: PaceWalking and Growing Older

Walter M. Bortz II, "Disuse and Aging." *Journal of the American Medical Association* (September 10, 1982), p. 1203.

Jane E. Brody, "Aging: Studies Point Toward Ways to Slow It." *New York Times* (June 10, 1986) p. C1.

———"Personal Health." *New York Times* (June 11, 1986), p. C2.

Council on Scientific Affairs, "Exercise Programs for the Elderly." *Journal of the American Medical Association* (July 27, 1984), p. 544.

Richard C. Crandall, "The Aged Athlete." *Running and Fitness* (1982).

John Jerome, "Don't Pity the Aged Runner." *Running* (July/August 1982), p. 26.

John Pocari, et al, "Is Fast Walking an Adequate Aerobic Training Stimulus for 30- to 69-Year-Old Men and Women?" *The Physician and Sportsmedicine* (February 1987), p. 119.

Kayleen Sager, "Exercises to Activate Seniors." *The Physician and Sportsmedicine* (May 1984), p. 144.

Sofia Shafquat, ed., "Attitude Adjustment," in "Health Watch." *Runner's World* (February 1987), p. 12.

Ernst L. Wynder and Marvin M. Kristein, "Suppose We Died Young, Late in Life . . .?" *Journal of the American Medical Association* 238 (1977), p. 1507.

Chapter 6: PaceWalking and Pregnancy

R. Artal (Mittlemark) and R.A. Wiswell, eds., *Exercise in Pregnancy.* Baltimore: Williams and Wilkins, 1986.

S. Burkhardt and S. Horowitz, "Walking Through Pregnancy." *The Walking Magazine* (December/January 1987), p. 73.

M.M. Gauthier, "Guidelines for Exercise During Pregnancy: Too Little or Too Much?" *The Physician and Sportsmedicine* (April 1986), p. 162.

J. Heinonen, "Running For Two." *Runner's World* (September 1985), p. 45.

B.B. Rote, "Exercise in Pregnancy—An Inside Look." *Wellness Management* 3, no. 1 (spring 1987).

Chapter 9: Exercise and Health

T.J. Bassler, "Body Build and Mortality." *Journal of the American Medical Association* 244 (1980), p. 1437.

————"Hazards of Restrictive Diets." (letter) *Journal of the American Medical Association* 252 (1984), p. 483.

S.N. Blair, et al, "Relationships Between Exercise or Physical Activity and Other Health Behaviors." *Public Health Reports* 100 (1985), p. 172.

Jane E. Brody, "Fitness: Is It Good For You?" *New York Times Good Health Magazine* (October 5, 1986), p. 26.

M. Castleman, "Can Running Improve Your Sex Life?" *Runner's World* (April 1985), p. 50.

Kenneth Cooper, *Running Without Fear*. New York: M. Evans and Co., 1985.

Council on Scientific Affairs, "Physician-Supervised Exercise Programs in Rehabilitation of Patients with Coronary Heart Disease." *Journal of the American Medical Association* 245 (1981), p. 1463.

"Easy Does It." *U.S. News & World Report* (August 11, 1986).

"Forum: Exercise and Health." *Preventive Medicine* (January 1984), p. 1–139.

H. Higdon, "High Success on Low Mileage." *The Runner* (March 1987), p. 40.

W.B. Kannel and P. Sorlie, "Some Health Benefits of Physical Activity: The Framingham Study." *Archives of Internal Medicine* 132 (1979), p. 857.

T.E. Kottke, "Exercise in the Management and Rehabilitation of Selected Chronic Diseases." *Preventive Medicine* 13 (1984), p. 47.

D.M. Kramsch, "Reduction of Coronary Atherosclerosis by Moderate Conditioning Exercise in Monkeys on an Atherogenic Diet." *New England Journal of Medicine* 305 (1981), p. 1483.

N.E. Lane, et al, "Long-Distance Running, Bone Density, and Osteoarthritis." *Journal of the American Medical Association* 255 (1986), p. 1147.

A.S. Leon, "Forum: Exercise and Health." *Preventive Medicine* 13 (1984), p. 1–99.

T. Monahan, "Exercise and Depression: Swapping Sweat for Serenity?" *The Physician and Sportsmedicine* (September 1986), p. 192.

A. Oberman, "Healthy Exercise." *Western Journal of Medicine* 141 (1984), p. 864.

R.S. Paffenbarger, "A Natural History of Athleticism and Cardiovascular Health." *Journal of the American Medical Association* 252 (1984), p. 491.

R.S. Paffenbarger and R.T. Hyde, "Exercise as a Protection Against Heart Attack." *New England Journal of Medicine* 302 (1980), p. 1026.

————"Exercise in the Prevention of Coronary Heart Disease." *Preventive Medicine* 13 (1984), p. 3.

R.S. Paffenbarger, et al., "Physical Activity, All-Cause Mortality, and Longevity of College Alumni." *New England Journal of Medicine* 314 (1986), p. 605.

R.S. Panush, et al. "Is Running Associated with Degenerative Joint Disease?" *Journal of the American Medical Association* 255 (1986), p. 1152.

R. Pollner, "Osteoporosis: Looking at the Whole Picture." *Medical World News* (January 14, 1985), p. 38.

"Protective Effect of Physical Activity on Coronary Heart Disease." *Morbidity and Mortality Weekly Report* 36 (July 10, 1987), p. 426.

A.H. Rosenstein, "The Benefits of Health Maintenance." *The Physician and Sportsmedicine* (April 1987), p. 57.

D.S. Siscovick, "The Incidence of Primary Cardiac Arrest During Vigorous Exercise." *New England Journal of Medicine* 311 (1984), p. 874.

D.S. Siscovick, et al, "The Disease-Specific Benefits and Risks of Physical Activity and Exercise." *Public Health Reports* 100 (1985), p. 180.

H. A. Solomon, *The Exercise Myth*. New York: Harcourt Brace Jovanovich, 1984.

F.A. Stutman, *Walk, Don't Die*. New York: Medical Manor Books, 1986.

G.S. Thomas, et al., *Exercise and Health*. Cambridge, Mass.: Oelgeschlager, Gunn, and Hain, 1981.

United States Public Health Service, "Workshop on the Epidemiologic and Public Health Aspects of Physical Activity and Exercise. *Public Health Reports* 100 (1985), p. 118–224.

S.P. Van Camp, "The Fixx Tragedy: A Cardiologist's Perspective." *The Physician and Sportsmedicine* (September 1984), p. 153.

Chapter 10: Nutrition and Weight Control for the PaceWalker

The American Heart Association Diet. Dallas: American Heart Association, 1985.

V. Aronson, *Thirty Days to Better Nutrition*. Englewood Cliffs, N.J.: Prentice-Hall, 1987.

"Biology, Culture, Dietary Changes Conspire to Increase Incidence of Obesity." Medical News and Perspectives. *Journal of the American Medical Association* 256 (1986), p. 2157.

Jane E. Brody, "Why Many Efforts Fail to Change Unhealthy Habits." *New York Times* (April 28, 1987), p. C1.

S.M. Grundy, "Rationale of the Diet-Heart Statement of the American Heart Association." *Circulation* 65 (1982), p. 839A.

S.L. Halpern, ed., *Clinical Nutrition*. Philadelphia: J.B. Lippincott, 1979.

M. Katahn, *The Rotation Diet*. New York: W.W. Norton, 1986.

"Metropolitan Height and Weight Tables." New York: Metropolitan Life Insurance Co., 1983.

"Obesity's Many Disorders." Medical News and Perspectives. *Journal of the American Medical Association* 256 (1986), p. 2301.

N. Pritikin, *The Pritikin Promise*. New York: Simon & Schuster, 1983.

B. Stamford, "What's the Importance of Percent Body Fat?" *The Physician and Sportsmedicine* (March 1987), p. 216.

"What Is the Difference Between Crude and Dietary Fiber?" *University of California, Berkeley, Wellness Letter* 3 (August 1987), p. 8.

Chapter 11: Conclusion

National Center for Health Statistics, *Advance Data* (September 19, 1986), pp. 2, 7.

APPENDIX 2

PaceWalking and the Literature—A Guide

This section contains the names of the books dealing with some other aerobic sports, and a few related items.

Running

Two of the best books are still those I used myself when I started running: Jim Fixx's *The Complete Book of Running* (New York: Random House, 1977) and *The Runner's Handbook* by Bob Glover and Jack Shepherd (New York: Viking, 1977). Another good book from that era is Joe Henderson's *Jog, Run, Race* (Mountain View, Calif., 1977). A fine contemporary book is (Jeff) *Galloway's Book on Running* (Bolinas, Calif.: Shelter Publications, 1984).

Swimming

There is one book that stands head and shoulders above the rest: Jane Katz's *Swimming for Total Fitness* (Garden City, N.Y.: Dolphin Books/Doubleday, 1981).

Cycling

In my view the bicycling equivalent of *The Complete Book of Running* has yet to be written. While you are waiting, two pretty good books on the subject are Thom Lieb's *Everybody's Book of Bicycle Riding* (Emmaus, Pa.: Rodale Press, 1981) and *Bill Walton's Total Book of Bicycling* (New York: Bantam Books, 1985).

Triathlon

On my own favorite endurance sport, for the beginners, novices, and middle- to back-of-the-packers among you, I recommend my own book, *Triathloning for Ordinary Mortals* (New York: W. W. Norton, 1986). If your aim is an Ironman triathlon, you can't do better than the first really good book published on the sport, Sally Edward's *Triathlon: A Triple Fitness Sport* (Sacramento, Calif.: Fleet Feet Press, 1982). For people who want to achieve top performance, a fine book that integrates a great deal of exercise physiology with a training program designed by one of the world's greatest triathletes is *Dave Scott's Triathlon Training* (New York: Fireside/Simon & Schuster, 1986). *Scott Tinley's Winning Triathlon*, also by one of the all-time greats, is similarly pitched toward achieving peak performance.

Health Concerns

The book on the subject is *Exercise and Health*, written by Gregory Thomas and his colleagues (Cambridge, Mass.: Oelgeschlager, Gunn & Hain, 1981). *The* book on nutrition is Virginia Aronson's *Thirty Days to Better Nutrition* (Englewood Cliffs, N.J.: Prentice-Hall, 1986). The one book on weight loss that I can recommend is Martin Katahn's *The Rotation Diet* (New York: W. W. Norton, 1986). Finally, if you are one of those rare people who get injured while PaceWalking, or one of those less-rare people who get injured doing one of the other aerobic sports, what better book is there to consult than *Peak Condition: Winning Strategies to Prevent, Treat, and Rehabilitate Sports Injuries,* by James Garrick, M.D., and Peter Radetsky (New York: Harper & Row, Publishers, 1988).

Magazines

There is (as of the summer of 1987) only one magazine devoted to walking: *The Walking Magazine* (Boston: Raben Publishing Co.). It covers all aspects of walking, including walking for aerobic exercise. It is lively and attractive. The leading running magazine is Rodale Press's *Runners' World*, and the leading cycling magazine is their *Bicycling*. There are two prominent triathlon monthlies: *Triathlete* and *Triathlon Today*.

APPENDIX 3

Guide to PaceWalking Opportunities

Walking Clubs and Organizations

There are numerous walking clubs in the United States. There are as many varieties of walking clubs as there are varieties of walking itself: walking for exercise like PaceWalking, leisure walking, hiking, race walking, backpacking and camping, wilderness walking, and orienteering.

The Walking Magazine regularly publishes a list of walking clubs from around the country. You can consult it for information on local clubs in your area. A few of the clubs and organizations with a more national focus are:

THE PREVENTION WALKING CLUB
33 East Minor Street
Emmaus, Pa. 18049

THE ROCKPORT WALKING INSTITUTE
P.O. Box 480
Marlboro, Mass. 01752

THE WALKWAYS CENTER
Suite 427
733 15th Street, NW
Washington, D.C. 20005

WALKABOUT INTERNATIONAL
P.O. Box 6540
San Diego, Calif. 92106

WALKERS CLUB OF AMERICA
Box M
Livingston Manor, N.Y. 12758

Finally, I have my own organization for the promotion of PaceWalking:

PACEWALKERS OF AMERICA™
Box QQ
East Setauket, N.Y. 11733

Where to PaceWalk:
Numbers to Call for Information

Alabama 800-252-2262
Alaska 907-465-2010
Arizona 602-255-3618
Arkansas 800-643-8383
    800-482-3999
California 916-322-1396
Colorado 800-255-5550
Connecticut 203-566-3948
Delaware 800-441-8846
    800-282-8667
Florida 904-487-1462
Georgia 404-656-3590
Hawaii 212-986-9203
    808-923-1811
Idaho 800-635-7820
    208-334-2470
Illinois 312-793-2094
Indiana 317-232-8860
Iowa 515-281-3100
Kansas 913-296-2009
Kentucky 800-225-8747
    502-564-4930
Louisiana 800-231-4730
    504-925-3860
Maine 207-289-2423
Maryland 301-269-3517
Massachusetts 617-727-3201
    617-727-3180
Michigan 517-373-1195
Minnesota 800-328-1461
    800-652-9747
Mississippi 800-647-2290
    800-962-2346

Missouri 314-751-4133
Montana 800-548-3390
    406-444-2654
Nebraska 800-228-4307
    800-742-7595
Nevada 702-885-4322
New Hampshire 603-271-2666
New Jersey 609-292-2470
New Mexico 800-545-2040
    505-827-0291
New York 518-474-4116
North Carolina 800-847-4862
North Dakota 800-437-2077
    800-472-2100
Ohio 614-466-8844
Oklahoma 405-521-2409
Oregon 800-547-7842
    800-233-3306
Pennsylvania 800-847-4872
Rhode Island 401-277-2601
South Carolina 803-734-0135
South Dakota 800-843-1930
Tennessee 615-741-2158
Texas 512-465-7401
Utah 801-533-5681
Vermont 802-828-3236
Virginia 804-786-4484
Washington 800-541-9274
    800-562-4570
West Virginia 800-225-5982
Wisconsin 608-266-2161
Wyoming 307-777-7777

Acknowledgments

*F*irst I would like to thank Betty Prashker, editor-in-chief at Crown, for taking on this book at a time when few publishers were doing books on health and fitness. I hope that her faith will be rewarded.

I would also like to thank my agent, Harvey Klinger, for his confidence, his hard work, his good humor, and his persistence. I would like to thank Betty in particular for insisting that I have a coauthor and Harvey for making the connection between me and Peter Radetsky. I have provided most of the thought for this book, but it is Peter who has provided most of the voice. And it is a voice that I don't have, as my previous books will attest: one that sings swiftly and brightly, with a beautiful economy of phrase. Peter is not only a fine writer, but also a delight to work with. I am sure that you have enjoyed his writing as much as I have.

Also at Crown, I want to thank our editor, Barbara Grossman, our production editor, Maria Bottino, and our publicist, Debbie Rubin, for their hard, professional work and dedication to this book.

As always on my exercise books, I must thank Charlie Ogilvie, D.O., who inspired me to take up exercise in the first place, an activity that has become such an important part of my life. Charlie's colleague and our friend at the Texas College of Osteopathic Medicine, Irvin "Kim" Korr, Ph.D., provided a great example of healthy living and a wonderful story, which I used in the book.

I thank my good friend and colleague Virginia Aronson, R.D., M.S., author and nutritionist, for her very helpful review of the chapter on nutrition.

I want to thank my department chairman, Dr. Andre Varma, of the Department of Community and Preventive Medicine, School of Medicine, State University of New York at Stony Brook, for his support and understanding of this project.

I thank Gary Westerfield, coach of the U.S. National Women's Race Walking Team, for helping me to better understand the race walking gait and for reviewing my description of the PaceWalking gait.

I thank David Balboa and Deena Karabell, of The Walking Center in New York City and developers of the Balboa Method of Fitness Walking, for their assistance on the PaceWalking technique.

I want to thank all of my friends in the wonderful sport of triathlon who have encouraged me to become an athlete.

Finally, I want to thank my dad, Professor Harold J. Jonas. Dad did not edit this book, but he has edited five of my previous six. In that process, he has helped me learn how to think and how to write. In that way, he helped me with this book, too.

Index